MW00623989

Amy Blackmarr

Dahlonega Haunts

Ghostly Adventures in a Georgia Mountain Town

(with R. Brian Keith, Psychic)
Photographs by Jack Anthony

Willacoochee Publishing Company
willapress@hotmail.com
www.amyblackmarr.com

First Edition
Second Corrected Printing

Book Design by Sarah McGhee
All Photos by Jack Anthony
except "ghostly roses" (stock photo), old Besser Hotel, and author photo.
— Emmet Fox is quoted from *Around the Year with Emmet Fox: a Book of Daily Readings*. New York: Harpercollins, 1992 —

PRINTED IN THE UNITED STATES OF AMERICA
EAN 978-0-9773173-0-1 / ISBN 0-9773173-0-7

Also by Amy Blackmarr

Going to Ground
House of Steps
Above the Fall Line

Willacoochee Publishing Company
willapress@hotmail.com
www.amyblackmarr.com

To Joe Stofiel

Warm and earnest thanks to my large-hearted psychic medicine-man friend R. Brian Keith for understanding, encouraging, supporting, and facilitating the greater purpose of this work despite much inconvenience to himself; Wendy McFarland, whose friendship and faith in me has been a source of encouragement and support for so long and in so many ways; Lou Ann Thomas, whose sense of humor buoyed me up at the most difficult times and whose editorial guidance was a great help; Sarah McGhee, who gave her abundant creative resources, originality, and energy to designing this book; Jack Anthony, for his unparalleled photographer's eye; Debra Capponi, Information Specialist for the Lumpkin County Library, for her invaluable last-minute assistance; Don and Kate McElliott at Quigley's Rare Books for their hard work with publishing, publicity, and support; Glenn Connor, for introducing me to local history, ghost stories, and townspeople (living and otherwise), and for sharing hours upon hours of his time and energy with me; Tommy Cobb, Bill Kinsland, Erin Riley, Jeff Weaver, Rick Whorf, Erin Peck, and the many other merchants, citizens, and friends of Dahlonega who shared their stories with me and then let me invade their privacy, their homes, their restaurants, and their shops; Rose Birdwell, Tom Stargel, and Maxwell Center, for their extremely helpful survey of Cane Creek Cemetery, and Rose Birdwell and Nema Mobley for their equally helpful survey of Mt. Hope Cemetery; Faye Buice and her daughter, Jane Echols, for sharing Jane's photographs with me during the earliest stages of planning the book; Anne Amerson, for her research into Dahlonega history and her friendship; the Southeast Society for Paranormal Research, for their efforts; Mom, for her ingenious and uncompromising editorial eye and for her love, lunches, and support; the Lumpkin County

Library staff, who listened to my early tales and shivered when appropriate; my many friends and other family members, who encourage and support me in uncounted generous ways; and my husband, Chase Anderson, who despite his own trials selflessly spent hundreds of hours helping me with all the parts of this project long before it ever became a book and then kept pushing me to keep it going when my energy flagged. Most importantly, to the spirits who stayed behind, and those who moved on into the light, for having the courage to take part in this most hopeful and remarkable of journeys . . . unending thanks. For all those stories that did not find their way into this book, and to anyone I've forgotten to mention, my apologies and heartfelt thanks.

"Amy, I have been taking some pictures for the book. Since I have been telling people what I am doing I have been introduced to several ghosts and I didn't know about any before: three at the Moore House (by the college), a persistent one at the hospital, and one in the basement of the college gym where they used to store cadavers for the physical therapy program. — Jack"

"Dear Jack. See? Ghosts are all over *Dahlonega. Please tell any I've left out (if you see them) that I'll try to work them in somehow. — Amy"*

If the doors of perception were cleansed everything would appear as it is: Infinite.

— William Blake
The Marriage of Heaven and Hell

"We've all heard stories of Beyond. Now and then I think that sometimes the world of the dead gets mixed up in the world of the living. . . . There isn't always an answer for everything."

— The Housekeeper in *The Others*
Alejándro Amenabar, Dir.

Contents

changing paths and the search for a psychic

We are living in a technological age, and they [paranormal investigators] think, or at least some of them that I've met, in all sincerity, that running around with Geiger counters and cameras and instruments that can measure cold spots will be the way to investigate a haunting or a ghost. That's bullshit . . . .[Y]ou're dealing with a human being, nothing more, nothing less.

— Dr. Hans Holzer
in a 2005 interview with Jeff Belanger

As a writer, I'm always teaching the importance of extinguishing boundaries. Life, I'm always saying, is about learning not to expect.

But the moment I started doing paranormal research, my plans began to change. I shouldn't have been so surprised: my life has often taken dramatic turns. It scares my family to death.

Yet this path seemed drastically different from others I've headed down. Certainly there was nothing in my history, other than a lifelong interest in all things extranormal, to suggest that my career as a nature writer would get hijacked by ghosts! But in October I'd seen the trailer for *White Noise*, a recent Hollywood flick based on electronic voice phenomena, or EVP. Although the hypothesis has never been proven, these unexpected voices found in recording media have long been thought by reputable researchers to be of paranormal origin.

Intrigued, I bought a cheap voice recorder at the Wal-Mart and started asking around Dahlonega's downtown Square for local "haunts." Meanwhile, I talked my husband, Chase Anderson, into some late-night excursions with me to nearby graveyards. I wanted to see if capturing EVP was as easy as it sounded. And that, I expected, would be that.

As the days passed and our recordings piled up, I became increasingly frustrated that I never heard anything on the tapes except my own voice asking questions and, occasionally, an unexplained clicking. But I was astonished by the number of tales I was being told about paranormal activity around town. Spatulas tipped themselves off griddles and clattered to the floor. Doors unlocked themselves and swung open. Figurines flung themselves off shelves and broke — or vanished, only to be discovered across the hall a few minutes later. Pepper mills wouldn't stay put. Chess pieces rearranged themselves. Pictures fell off walls. Invisible fingers tapped shoulders and pressed sleeping tenants down in their beds and grasped bare arms in unlighted hallways. Kitchens were the center of so much activity that I wondered if Dahlonega simply possessed one very active Kitchen Ghost who craved attention. And there was more.

Dahlonega had a rich history — of gold miners and shootouts, gamblers and brothels, Cherokee Indians and the Appalachian Trail — but had yet to publish a collection of its own ghost stories. I decided to prove that this tiny mountain town was every bit Savannah's equal in the Georgia ghost business.

Meanwhile, I began reading in the field of paranormal science and found that the prevailing wisdom of scores of researchers and psychics — forensic psychologist Dr. Katherine Ramsland, for one; paranormal scientist Dr. Hans Holzer; well-known psychics Sybil Leek, James van Praagh, Sylvia Browne — clearly held that ghosts are people, too. Just because they'd "dropped their bodies," as the Eastern mystics put it, didn't mean they'd stopped existing altogether. There was just nothing material to house them in, make them dense and sluggish and . . . yes, visible.

More importantly, I began to wonder whether I had a responsibility to these "ghosts" beyond the simple telling of their stories. For if it *were* true that a ghost was, as most experts seemed to think, the essential conscious *beingness* of someone trapped because he didn't know he had died, or because he had developed an unhealthy attachment to the material world, then perhaps I had an obligation to let him know he didn't have to stay stuck. He could go on to the next stage of his evolutionary journey. To ignore his plight might be the equivalent of leaving a wounded man to die on the side of the road.

But heaven knows *I* was not the person to convey information to a ghost. Try as I might, I had never felt a cold spot nor seen any white mist nor heard a ghostly voice whispering in my ear. So I decided to find a medium. I would take him with me to the haunted places in Dahlonega so he could tell the ghost whatever he needed to know and (a bonus!) extract the real ghost story from the ghost himself.

I wouldn't offer to pay a dime, figuring this would help winnow out frauds.

I was skeptical when I first heard about Brian Keith. The man was not local, but came from halfway across the state to counsel clients in Dahlonega. He was half Blackfoot, almost seven feet tall, and adept in the "mantic arts." I'd had some bad experiences with so-called medicine men, and I'd gotten over my New Age fanaticism years ago. Now I was rabidly averse to anything that resembled it. The day I met Brian, all my red flags were up.

Brian's office in Dahlonega was dimly lighted and smelled of incense, and all manner of paraphernalia — enormous amethysts, quartz crystals, feathers, rattles, and heaven knows what else — was spread out on a table. I sat down, but inwardly I was rolling my eyes and shaking my head, thinking, Oh Lord, what have I gotten myself into now.

Although I had not spoken with Brian myself, I had told the woman who scheduled our appointment that I was writing a book of Dahlonega ghost stories and looking for a medium to convey information to the spirits. I told her I felt there might be a moral obligation involved.

"What are your credentials, Brian?" I asked, noticing how comfortable he seemed despite my obvious cautiousness.

"I'm a Georgia board-licensed counselor and therapist. I'm an internationally registered channel and medium. I'm an internationally registered metaphysician. And I've been in private counseling practice fifteen years."

"How did you discover you were psychic?"

"When I was three or four years old I began talking to and seeing people nobody else seemed to see or hear."

"So it was like the movie *The Sixth Sense*, where Cole tells Bruce Willis '*I see dead people all the time! They're everywhere!*'"

"It was exactly like that!" Brian said, laughing.

"Is that a true movie?"

"In its most basic sense. It is a gift. You *can* see them: there are invisible people wandering around who don't know they're dead. But the horrible looking ghosts, the vomit — all of that is Hollywood. The spiritual realm does not have special effects."

"That's a relief!"

"Yes it is, for all of us who do this work!"

"Is there a history of this gift in your family?"

"I come from a long line of Italian women on my maternal grandmother's side known as the Strega, a group of witches with medieval origins — but not 'witch' like the evil crones that ride broomsticks; the word is wych, meaning to twist, to bend, and to shift. Very early on they discovered which of us had the gift, and they began leading us along that pathway, sharing what they knew. Paranormal phenomena were commonplace while I was growing up. My maternal grandfather was full-blooded Blackfoot. Siksika. From Montana."

"Any other relevant history?"

"My Christian background is Baptist. In my early twenties I went into the Pentecostal movement, then into the Full Gospel movement — the Charismatic movement. There, my gifts were called the Word of Wisdom, the Word of Knowledge, and the Discernment of Spirit. That was my early history."

Now the critical question: "Why do you contact spirits?"

"It's part of my service on earth," he said. "People who are stuck between the worlds are very limited, because not many people on earth will access the psychic gift. So if I find a person trapped, I try to help. The only difference between you living and you dead is that you don't have a physical body: otherwise you're exactly the same."

So Brian professed to be an altruist, I thought. We'll see if he asks for money.

During the half-hour that followed, I explained how my concept of the book had changed, and Brian offered without qualification to help in any way I might need him. He believed I was hearing these particular stories because they wanted to be told. He said I was a "bridge-builder" and had been "called" by the spirits to write this book for a whole host of spiritual reasons having to do with raising consciousness on the planet. He had already consulted his "guides" and been advised to help me.

"How would you feel if I decided not to use your name in the book, but just report on your readings?"

He shrugged. "You're the writer. I'm just here to do my work and it's clear to me that Spirit wants this work to be done."

By the time I left Brian's office, even though I wasn't convinced of the auspicious role he thought I was supposed to play, I was struck by his conviction about his own purpose. "I know who I am," he had said when I challenged his vanity. And I believed he was truly open, kind-hearted, and in earnest. The subject of money had never come up. That was enough for me.

Over the months that followed, I escorted Brian around "haunted" Dahlonega, and he conducted on-site psi sessions (psychic sessions), or readings, so we could learn why the ghosts were there. In some cases, when it was their desire, Brian helped them "cross over" to the Other Side. He handled this situation in much the same way I expect he handles his counseling practice: by helping the spirit let go of fear, guilt, sadness, or other attachments it had formed with its former human identity.

In cases where the spirit could not be reached, Brian prayed for angelic intervention and moved on.

In cases where the spirit expressed no interest in going on, we left it where it was.

The stories that follow tell the tales I heard from local townspeople, describe the scant bit of "hard" evidence that came my way in the form of my own EVP recordings, and give Brian's interpretation of the psychic information he received in his readings. I have also included relevant bits from ongoing interviews with him about his take on spiritual matters.

I should mention that because Brian is a psychic first and a medium second, when he conducted his readings he didn't do any of the things I expected mediums to do. His voice didn't change. He didn't step psychically aside and become a channel, allowing "the entity" to use his vocal chords to talk. Instead, he worked on an intuitive level — which means that Brian himself remained present while he reported to me his interpretation of the entity's thoughts and feelings. This often made me wonder how much of Brian himself was mixed up in his readings, and I was never reticent about telling him so. He was a tremendously good sport about it.

ghostly roses

I will be the first to admit that until I began work on this book, my experiences with the paranormal had been mostly vicarious. In all my life, despite my many attempts to leave my body and fly to Russia, read minds, bend spoons, levitate, cast spells, commune with spirits, and channel literary masterpieces, I had never seen a ghost. I had never talked to a ghost. I had never watched a wine glass float across a room nor felt a ghostly tug at my skirts. If a room full of ghosts had been having a cocktail party right here in my den, I would not have heard the orchestra playing.

The catalog of what I suspect were my authentic experiences with ghosts was limited to two. When I was a teenager, I awoke to the sound of our French doors opening and the certainty that someone was standing at the foot of my bed. A woman's voice, very loud, sounded in my head: "It's all right, honey; it's only your Pop." Pop was my grandfather, and considering he had died a few days earlier, this incident doesn't seem all that strange. And ten years ago when I was living in Pop's South-Georgia cabin, I awoke to a rustling sound and realized that the evil Spanish woman I had just been dreaming of — a terrifying figure wearing a black mantilla and dressed head to toe in black lace — was gliding toward my bed. She raised her hand and spoke — I no longer remember the words — and at that instant the phone rang and she vanished. I glanced at the clock: it was 4 a.m. I answered, but heard only the static of an open line. Maybe I made up the evil Spanish woman, but I think a ghost made the phone call.

I don't know why I was never "sensitive." I wanted to be. Oh, I got goose bumps like everybody else and occasional waves of free-floating emotion, but that seemed like hormones to me.

The Dahlonega First Baptist Church is an enormous brick structure on a hill overlooking the downtown Square — one pastor I know calls it Fort God. I attended a noon Alzheimer's support group meeting there and as I approached the door downstairs was overwhelmed by the scent of roses. I looked around for a rose bush, but saw none. Besides, it was mid-December and had been appallingly cold for weeks.

I went on to the meeting, stayed until around two, then left the building from the same door I'd entered. Halfway to my car I noticed it again: roses. I searched the parking lot, even walked around the corner of the building, in case a funeral had taken place and left a lingering scent. But I saw no flowers, only the large paved lot and half a dozen vehicles. I left, thinking the incident curious. Then I went to work and forgot about it.

Later that evening I was having supper at Wylie's Restaurant and ran into Bogy Patton. Bogy grew up in

Dahlonega. I told him I was working on this book and to my surprise, he said, "Well, you should check out the Baptist Church."

I was instantly attentive. "Why?"

"There used to be an old house there. Two crazy sisters lived in it. People said the place was haunted."

"Haunted by who?"

"I don't know. We used to run up on the porch, knock on the door, and hide."

"They didn't by any chance have a garden, did they?"

"A rose garden," Bogy said.

"No!"

"Oh yes they did. You used to see one of the sisters out there all the time."

I told Bogy I'd smelled roses at the church earlier that day and asked if he knew the family name or where the garden had been, but he couldn't remember.

Around nine, I stopped by the church on my way home. I walked all around the parking lot, but the scent of roses was gone.

Still, I was thrilled! I told my tale all over the place. "I've had an Authentic Paranormal Experience!" I said, and we all shuddered.

When Saturday night arrived, I took my little recorder for capturing EVP, my husband, and our friend Jeff Weaver back to the Baptist church. Jeff had told us he was a little psychic and, like me, was fascinated by EVP. The building was dark and unoccupied. We stood outside in the freezing cold while I, feeling silly, tossed questions into the air — "Is anyone here?" . . . "Do you want to talk?" . . . "Can you say your name?" — and waited for a ghost to answer.

Meanwhile, Jeff said he had seen (in his mind's eye) an old woman, small, with a bent back, gray hair, and glasses.

He asked me what the sisters looked like, but I didn't

know. He soon left, and Chase and I didn't stay much longer, but at the door near where I'd smelled the roses, I turned on the recorder a final time and said: "If you're here, will you give us a sign?" Immediately two metallic cracks sounded just above my head — and then a third, from the hall behind the door. Chase and I stared at each other. "Did you hear that?" I said.

"That was wild!" said Chase.

I asked a few more questions, and we left, pretty well spooked.

At home, I listened to the recording again, with headphones. I heard the three loud cracks . . . along with cars going by, dogs barking, doors slamming, and people yelling in the distance. In the end, we decided the noises were from building stress caused by the cold, or maybe something knocking against a gutter. It was just impossible to be certain, which is the problem with most "hard" data in this sort of research.

But I was really excited now, and convinced *something* was there. So Sunday afternoon, back I went to the church to try again to record the ghost on tape.

The cold was bitter, and in anticipation of recording EVP in cemeteries all day I wore a thick sweater and my down vest, a scarf, gloves, stocking cap, boots, jeans, and even long underwear, and I was loaded down with notebook and pen, recorder and headphones, and a basket with a flashlight and spare batteries. I felt goofy and eccentric and prayed no one would "catch" me — what on earth would I *say*? "Hey, don't mind me. I'm just trying to get a ghost to talk on my recorder."

And as the devil would have it, the minute I slammed the car door and started toward the building, out came a Baptist with a frown on his face.

I blundered straight into my confession. "Hey!" I said

cheerily, and gabbled on. "It's okay. I'm not here to steal anything. Ha-ha. I'm writing a book of Dahlonega ghost stories and I'm doing a little research. Ah . . . I'm not actually a nut."

"Oh," said the Baptist.

Quickly I told him how I'd smelled roses a few days earlier and that I wanted to find out more. "Was there a funeral recently or anything where there might have been roses?"

He pointed to a vent eight feet up in the brick wall, near the door. "That vent goes into the sanctuary," he said. "We always have flowers in there." He smiled.

I stood under the vent and, to my chagrin, the scent of hothouse flowers wafted downward onto the top of my head. "That's probably all it was," I said, disappointed (but not entirely convinced).

"We had these trees cut back a few days ago." He indicated some evergreens in the parking lot, the shrubbery near the door.

"Are those tea olives?"

"I don't know. But that might be what you smelled."

"Yeah, that was probably it," I said, so embarrassed I just thanked him and left.

It was a long time before I was able to learn anything more about the sisters, whose name, I finally discovered, was Gaillard. Meanwhile, my thrill about those invisible roses was playing a big part in my excitement about the book I wanted to write, and I became an even more avid collector of EVP.

Then I met Glenn Connor, a local resident well-versed in local color, and he remembered the sisters. "Did they have a rose garden?" was the first question out of my mouth.

"I don't remember a rose garden. Miss Sallie was one of the sisters. The house burned."

"You don't remember a garden of any kind?" I pressed.

"No. That was a haunted house, though. Professor Gaillard came to the college about the time it was founded in the early 1870s, stayed there sixty years. He had two girls and maybe one or two boys. One of the boys was a lawyer. I remember him walking around here when I was a kid, top hat on. He was kind of a peculiar person, too. And those two ladies up there, they were just flat crazy."

"Were they twins?"

"No. I saw them sometimes, but my mother said not to go up there. She said they were witches. I just stayed away from them." He stopped, then looked up and said cheerfully, "We've had some extremely interesting people here in Dahlonega!"

Months later, local historian Anne Amerson called me on the phone after she had read an early draft of this story. "Amy," she said. "You mean nobody ever told you the locals have always called that place *Rose Hill*?"

the haunted town

"Brian, why does Dahlonega have such a concentration of paranormal activity?"

"Sometimes places are built over burial grounds — or in the case of Dahlonega it's because of the large amount of gold and crystals here. Anywhere you have gold and crystals you have a perfect matrix. Gold is the highest vibrating thing on earth. That's one reason wedding bands are made of gold. Gold activates things. Anywhere there's a large collection of gold or crystals in the soil, spirits find it very easy to maintain energy."

— Brian Keith
in an interview with the author

Many of us have forgotten that North Georgia — not California — was the site of the first gold rush in this country. In fact, gold was mined in North Carolina as early as 1799, and some believe the first discovery of Georgia gold by white men was on Duke's Creek in White County in 1829, long before prospectors rushed off to California. Contrarily, Dahlonega legend holds with its own old Ben Parks, who claimed that early in 1828 he kicked over a rock while he was deer hunting, found it laced with gold, and word got around so fast that it initiated the surge of miners into North Georgia.

Either way, when the governor of Georgia partitioned the vast Cherokee lands to give to Revolutionary War veterans and their widows in the 1832 lottery, prospectors quickly bought up the lots, and the Georgia gold rush hit its peak. Auraria, now a ghost town a few miles south of Dahlonega between the Chestatee and Etowah rivers, sprang up to support the mining community. Dahlonega quickly followed. The Cherokee Indians, who had been living on the land for centuries, were removed and escorted to Oklahoma. Their tragic journey became known as the Trail of Tears.

Ironically, the word "Dahlonega" is a corruption of the original Cherokee word for *yellow*, and it has long been established that the Indians knew about the gold here long before white men "discovered" it. The attitudes of early traders gave them ample reason to keep the knowledge secret. Unfortunately the secret could only delay, but not prevent, the native people's dislocation.

Bill Kinsland is an authority on early Dahlonega history. "This was Cherokee land," he said one day as we stood in his Hometown Book Store on the Square. "The Cherokees actually had a village right in this area, in 1832, when the first surveys were done."

"Where was the village?"

"It wasn't an organized town as such, but more like little farms and cabins. If you go back to the 1832 survey, that surveyor was required to make a note of 'Cherokee improvements' on each land lot, and that meant farmhouses, pig sties, barns, mills, all that sort of thing. There was quite a bit of that around here. Chestatee Old Town was on the other side of Crown Mountain down by the river. The Cherokees had a voting place there for the Cherokee nation."

"Why do you think I haven't found any Cherokee ghosts, Bill?" I said. "It seems like everything is connected with Anglo-Saxon history."

"There were many campfires here before ours," Bill said, nodding.

"And something about Dahlonega draws people," I went on. "Several people have told me that after they came here the first time they felt an unexpected affinity for the area, and it influenced them to move here." In fact, many people I knew in Dahlonega were not even native Southerners, but from the Midwest or Northeast.

"It's true," said Bill, and he recalled an afternoon when a couple rushed into his store in a panic. The woman was weeping inconsolably, and the man was at a complete loss to understand why. They'd stopped at the Welcome Center, and the staff had sent them to Bill because of his knowledge of town history.

"They were just your ordinary Anglo-Saxon Protestant middle-class never-get-involved-in-anything-weird-or-psychic types," Bill said, "and they'd been up in North Carolina visiting and thought they'd take a detour through North Georgia. They'd never been to Dahlonega before, just saw it on the map and thought they'd see what all this was over here. They were coming through the Square when all of a sudden this lady breaks out into tears and has a sudden panic reaction and deep sadness and all these horrible emotions. They can't figure it out. She has a feeling of having been here before — *déjà vu* big-time — and she starts looking around for this old house. It had two stories and dormers across the top — and the more she described it, the more I realized she was talking about the old Hughes-Moore house."

The woman had a vivid memory of being taken as a child to kiss an old woman who was laid out in a coffin in the house. She felt a tremendous sadness; yet she'd never heard of Dahlonega in her life, and the place had been torn down in the Forties. When Bill was able to tell her a little about the house, she finally stopped crying, and the couple left town. Bill hadn't seen them since.

"Probably spooked them too bad!" I said.

"I'm sure it scared the pee-wally-ding-dong out of them, you know, never having thought about such things. They just walked right through a time warp or something."

The Psychic Scoop on Native American Haunts

"Brian, why haven't I come across any Native American hauntings?" I asked during one of our many conversations.

"Because Native Americans do not haunt. They know that this is not their home, that they only make a stop here before they return to their ancestors. When they pass over, they're prepared for it. They know what to expect. It's talked about from the day they're born. Death is an accepted part of their lives. In white culture, death is taboo. We don't talk about it because it's so uncomfortable, so when we die, we don't know what to do, don't have any connection. One reason ghosts get stuck is that they don't have a clue how to go on."

Lumpkin County Courthouse, with bricks containing gold

the ghost
in the old courthouse

The oldest building on the Square, the Lumpkin County courthouse, was built in 1836 from local brick that contains traces of Dahlonega gold, which is known to be some of the purest in the world. Now the bottom floor houses a museum featuring gold technology and coins minted at the federal branch mint, which operated in Dahlonega from 1838 until it was taken over by the Confederacy in 1861, when Georgia seceded from the Union. A film about local gold-mining history is shown upstairs in the old courtroom.

Sharon Johnson, the museum's manager, and I were in the main lobby talking about the courthouse ghost, whom the staff affectionately call "Tommy."

"People say a tall figure in a hooded robe has been seen in the windows and hanging out on the balcony," I told Sharon, "and I heard something about a knocking sound inside the walls. You've been here a long time, Sharon. Have you ever seen anything?"

"Once in a while before the carpet was installed upstairs I'd think I heard someone walking around up there. But the only real eerie thing that has ever happened to me — and this has been recently — is when the stamp mill came on by itself."

(In the early days of gold mining, devices powered by steam or water had "stamps" resembling pile drivers that pounded ore into powder so the gold could be separated. The museum had a small working electric mill.)

"There is no way that stamp mill can come on without somebody pushing that button," Sharon said. "Teresa was here that day and I said, 'Oh, I didn't know there was somebody in the museum.' She said, 'There's not.' Well, the stamp mill was just running away. And I said, 'There's got to be!' So I walked back there in the mining room and looked everywhere — I mean, there's no way even the smallest person could hide. I went in the mint room. There was nobody there."

"What did you do?"

"I just let it keep running. I can show you the toggle switch on it. There is no way . . ."

We walked back to the mining room so Sharon could show me the stamp mill. I flipped the toggle switch myself, but it took an effort. "How on earth?"

"I don't know. But things come up missing, too, and the staff will say, 'Well, Tommy got in again.'"

"Do the things show up again later?"

"Oh, yeah. I've had other staff who've had 'feelings.' We know that at least one man died here. We know there was an argument on the balcony and one man shoved another one."

Sharon took me upstairs to the jury room, showed me

Courtroom where a ghostly judge still presides

some of the bricks with gold in them, gave me a tour of the attic, and brought me back down to the second floor.

"I expect this place was the scene of more than one argument over the years," I said.

We were standing there talking, when all of a sudden from inside the courtroom — *BANG!*

"What was *that*?" I said.

"I don't know!" Sharon walked into the courtroom and looked around.

"It was a pop!"

"Tommy doesn't like us being up here!"

I held up my recorder. "This is supposed to record ghost voices."

"Did you have it on?"

"Yes! Let's see." I played the tape back and heard our conversation and the explosion, but no voices. Meanwhile, Sharon went to examine the projector and discovered the bulb was blown. "But the projector wasn't on, Sharon," I said.

"I know!"

"Want to try some EVP? We turn on the recorder and introduce ourselves and then we say, 'Hey, whoever you are. Is there something you want to say?' And then we wait and see if he says anything back."

Sharon shot me a curious look. "You mean you can hear him answer?"

"Well, no, not right then. But theoretically, if somebody's willing to talk, then when we play the tape back we can hear it. It's like a dog whistle. The sound is outside the normal human hearing frequency, but the recorder can pick it up."

"Oh."

"Okay, I'm just going to say it: Is anybody here?" Silence. "Is there anything you want to say?"

I waited a few seconds, then played the tape back.

The first question came. No response.

The second question came, and then — *STOMP!* If some man had been upstairs I'd have sworn he had stamped on the courtroom's wood floor.

Sharon and I stared at each other. "Did you hear that?" I said.

"I heard it! What *was* it?"

"I have no idea." I played the tape back several times, but all we could do was shake our heads in wonder.

I was thrilled. I counted the recording my first authentic EVP. It was only a stomp, but I hadn't made it, Sharon hadn't made it, and there was nobody upstairs (that we could see!) but us.

The Psychic Scoop

Brian and I stood outside the courthouse looking up at the second-floor windows. I had asked him if he could

Judge's chambers

tell me anything about the ghost called "Tommy." Now I turned on my recorder and waited while he "tuned in" to the presence in the courthouse.

Presently, Brian said, "I feel there was one particular judge who presided over this place in its glory, and he's very possessive about *his* courtroom. He's the one who was stomping around upstairs. He likes the second floor. Is the courtroom up there?"

"Yes. What about the light bulb?" I had told Brian about the EVP.

"That was him, too. I feel that this man favors the back of the building facing Dante's Café and that side of the Square. This is *his* building. He was the *judge*. That's his attitude. He's *the* ghost here."

"So a judge haunts the courthouse. That's pretty unoriginal, Brian."

"Were you expecting someone else?"

"Well . . . hmm. I get your point." Why had I expected anything different? "What about EVP? Do you think ghosts can really talk on tape?"

"Oh yes. It's all bioelectric energy, so recording devices can pick up those sounds. Ghosts or spirits leave light, happy messages. They like communicating. But when people pick up scary, malevolent voices, they're not really getting a person; they're getting a person's psychic residue or 'elemental.' An elemental is created out of the energy that comes from someone's very intense negative feelings and thoughts, and it can remain behind even after its 'owner' departs for the other world."

"Is an elemental limited in any way?"

"An elemental knows only to haunt. It searches for a place or person with the same kind of energy as the one who created it because it sustains itself on that energy."

"That sounds like a vampire!"

Brian laughed. "Well, in a way. When you read about a scary haunting, that's an elemental working on fear, so it has this scary quality. Elementals exist on negative emotion because that's what formed them."

"The judge isn't an elemental, though."

"No. He's just a spirit who's very possessive. These old men of Dahlonega really have a feeling of ownership."

"What old men?"

"Just you wait, dear. You'll see!"

Crisson Mine tunnel entrance (right)

the murders
on Bearden's Bridge Hill

The fall day was cool and clear when Solomon Stanberry, Iley Stuart, and James Witt rode through the valley to the forge at Louis Vanzant's farm on the Toccoa River in Dial, Georgia. Part of a company of irregulars, the men were on their way to muster into the Union Army in Cleveland, Tennessee, when they stopped at Vanzant's to have their horses shod.

But trouble was hot on their trail. A Confederate Home Guard unit — Findley's regiment from Dahlonega — had got wind that the men were up in Fannin County and tracked them down at the forge. In a matter of minutes the troops surrounded the place, took the three men prisoner, and brought them back to Dahlonega, where they were locked in an upstairs room of the courthouse and kept awaiting...what?

It was 1864. Sherman had set fire to Atlanta, and Confederate morale was crumbling. Yankees were crawling through Georgia, and tempers, and spirits, were breaking. Justice was uncertain and swift.

It seems no great surprise, then, to learn that four Confederates took the three Federals out late on a cold October night and set them on a forced march five miles east and over the covered bridge to Bearden's Bridge Hill. The moon was high and full, silvering the trees that stood in silent witness as, according to testimony from U.S. Army court martial records from 1865, the prisoners were forced down into a shallow pit and, for reasons now lost to history, shot to death.

One of the Confederates was William Reese Crisson, then a 1st Sergeant in Findley's 4th Regiment, 2nd Brigade — and founder of the Crisson gold mine in Dahlonega.

I was leaning on the counter in Bill Kinsland's book store while he related this bit of history, which he had learned from researching the murders for an article he and Jimmy Anderson had written years ago.

"But we didn't know anything about the court martial," Bill went on, "until years after our article came out, when a dear friend of mine who practically lived in the National Archives knocked over a box of old papers and discovered Crisson's name in the documents."

"But why did the court martial transcript matter so much?" I said.

"Because the court martial took place right after the murders. We had been working from the pension records of the widows, which were filed thirteen years later. So when Jimmy and I went out to Bearden's Bridge Hill to take pictures and look around, I kept wondering exactly where the men were shot, because we couldn't tell from the pension records. I started walking down the slope, and all of a sudden it hit me like a ton of bricks. The blood went out of my head and I started panicking and sweating."

"Your body somehow knew where those guys were murdered?"

He nodded. "Even though we had no documentary confirmation at the time. Then years later Bob found the court martial documents, and one witness talked about how they'd gotten these three irregulars down into a shallow pit in the side of the hill. Well, that's *exactly* where I was when the panic hit me." He shook his head. "I'll never forget that feeling. It was an anxiety attack, I suppose. It was a very scary experience."

The Psychic Scoop from the Crisson Gold Mine

Established by Crisson in 1847 — long before the Bearden's Bridge Hill murders — the Crisson Gold Mine was an open pit gold mine worked commercially until the early Eighties. I drove Brian out there one afternoon to find out whether, given Crisson's involvement in such a tragedy, his ghost might still be around, feeling regretful. I had given Brian the names of the three murdered men and the general time period but told him none of the details except to mention Crisson. I had said nothing about Bill Kinsland's experience.

We were approaching the building when Brian whistled. "It must have been awful the way these boys died, or they must have seen it coming. Because I feel pure, unadulterated terror. Iley Stuart, no vibrations. Solomon Stanberry suffered the most. And James Witt is here. It was awful." Brian frowned. "They really brutalized these men."

"I don't know anything about that, Brian."

"Crisson is here. See the way that column is tilted away from the building? Remember when I told you how in graveyards they put headstones down to make sure spirits

Tilted column, indicating a ghostly presence

stayed in, and when the spirit left its grave, the stone would tilt or fall?"

"I don't remember that at all."

"That's how you can tell if the spirit is still in its grave. The headstone is up."

"Oh, come on, Brian. I can't buy that."

"That's why headstones were put on graves."

"But if the ground gets wet and sinks —"

"Nothing happens by coincidence on earth. When something is set to go a certain way and it changes, that's a sign. Those bricks right there tell me something's off. Crisson is here. He was caught up in a kind of righteous fervor when they murdered those men, and later on he was traumatized by what he'd done. That's why his soul doesn't rest. Those men were waiting in terror. They were brutalized before they were finally shot and put out of their misery, and Solomon was the last one to die. He had to watch the other two be killed. Crisson is bound here because of how he murdered those men. He can't let it go."

"Is there anything we can do?"

Brian shook his head. "This is his personal hell. He's doing this knowingly; it's his idea."

I found this idea shocking, that a person would deliberately create his own hell by reliving his victim's terror. I couldn't say I believed Brian, but I could imagine that, if that *were* the case, it would certainly be effective. I've done some things to people I'd be horrified to relive from their point of view. I said, "So when you told me that ghosts have free will —"

"— they can even create their own version of hell. Free will is a universal principle. The only ones who don't have free will are angels."

"Because they're created —"

"— for a purpose." Brian paused. "But you can tell Mr. Crisson is a southern gentleman. He came up and acknowledged we were here."

"He did? Why didn't I feel anything?"

"Because you close yourself off."

"But I don't *feel* like I close myself off," I complained.

"I saw him standing by the door there."

"So Stanberry and Witt aren't here after all?" I said, wondering if I'd just caught Brian in a contradiction.

"That was a psychic imprint, a vibration that comes from emotional energy so intense it leaves a kind of permanent psychic footprint. See, Crisson is feeling *their* terror."

"Well how long will he keep putting himself through this?"

"Until he's able to see the light and realize that Christ's sacrifice has paid for this. But all kinds of spiritual teachers come here and talk to him. Jesus himself talks to him."

"Oh please, Brian. Jesus?"

"It's true. But Crisson is too stubborn. He's very dogmatic. That's why he thought he was right to butcher those men. Because they were *butchered*. 'Murdered' is a nice term for what was done to them."

Brian fell quiet a minute.

"What we *can* do," he went on, "is pray that the violet light of transmutation engulf this entire thing and bring healing. We can leave it in the hands of St. Germain. He works with calcified, hopeless situations. He works with the avatars to take the earth out of its negative, locked-in-the-physical existence to bring back the integration with spirit. His tool is the violet flame of transmutation, which carries mercy, forgiveness, and freedom."

This sounded like New Age claptrap to me. "*Really*, Brian," I said, not very sweetly.

"It's like changing venom into antivenom," he said. "It's like applying heat, and the heat causes such a chemical change that the poison is converted to medicine. When you find situations like this, you leave the flame, knowing that it won't stop burning until healing comes." After a minute, he looked at me. "This is done."

The Scoop on the Psychic Scoop

Months later I read that the color violet has the highest frequency in the visible spectrum, so it exists at the point of transition to the next octave of light. To the ancients, this transcendental color was a spiritual, rather than a physical, phenomenon.

St. Germain was a 16th century Renaissance man, friend of Rousseau and Voltaire. A master violinist, swordsman, and painter, with an extensive knowledge of herbalism and alchemy, some believe he was an ascended master who lived for nearly four centuries and was instrumental in raising human consciousness throughout the world.

Consolidated Mining Company, where ghosts gather

Hiram's fatal mistake

The next world is actually all around us here. The so-called dead are carrying on their lives here where we are now, but in their own world and in their own way. The reason we do not see them around us or collide with them is the same reason that one radio program does not interfere with another — they are on different wavelengths.

— Emmet Fox
Around the Year with Emmet Fox

From its opening in 1900 until it was sold at a devastating loss in 1906, the Dahlonega Consolidated Mining Company operated the largest gold plant ever constructed east of the Mississippi River, incorporating more than a dozen mines and nearly six hundred feet of tunnels. Gold mining was a dangerous operation, involving darkness, tons of water, and enormous machines that crushed rock and pulverized ore. Given the peril that miners faced, I expected the Consolidated to be thronging with ghosts. But the only story I dug up was from Hop Smith, a long-time guide, who said that two psychics on separate occasions had "seen" a man who had died in a mining accident. One of them said the man had taken two of his friends with him and his name sounded like "Hiram."

The Psychic Scoop from the Gold Mine

I took Brian to the Consolidated near dusk on a cool evening in May. The mine had closed by the time we arrived, so we stood outside the gift shop, which housed the entrance to the tunnels.

Brian stood silent a moment, then winced and clasped his abdomen.

"What is it?" I said, appalled. "Are you okay?" I was afraid he was having some sort of attack.

"What I feel here — I get a real sick feeling. Very confused. Awful."

"Lord. Is that what happens when you identify with a spirit?"

"Yes. I can feel what they felt. And this person was in terrible pain. I feel he has mistaken this place."

"Mistaken it how?"

"He came to the wrong place, got it mixed up with somewhere else. I don't know if it was something that stood here before the mine, or if it was somebody that worked the mine, but there's real confusion and a sense of helplessness. This man is stuck here, doesn't know where else to go. Doesn't know what happened."

"What *did* happen?"

"He had some kind of accident."

"Nobody knows of any record of deaths here."

"There might not be a record, but there's been a death on this place."

"When was it? Can you tell?"

"Late 1800s. It was almost like he was gored. Maybe he fell on something. But it was right here."

"Why did that psychic say he took his friends with him?"

"I think her story's right but it's a little mixed up. He was meeting friends. Maybe they were supposed to go hunting and he came to the wrong place, because his friends were not here. He never saw them. And he was either gored . . . it's *big*. Like he fell on a board! He wasn't down in the mine. He was up here. He is really confused. I'm going to tell him he can go to where his friends are."

Brian spent a few minutes going through a kind of ceremony that involved having Hiram acknowledge that he wanted to "cross over" to the Other Side; then Brian sent him onward with a blessing. He used the language of Christianity — priesthood, Heaven and Hell, the Holy Spirit, Christ, God the Father — and this made me uncomfortable because I didn't believe spiritual matters were limited to any particular religious doctrine.

"Why don't you use secular language?" I asked Brian. "Or Buddhist? Or anything else?"

"Because the symbology of Christianity is so rich with archetypes that stand for universal principles," he explained. "Even non-Christians understand the principle behind the word *Satan*."

"So it's semantics."

"And Christians have a language of love."

"I can buy that."

That Brian's version of Hiram's story was so different from the one Hop had told me surprised me, but then I was taking all of this ghost business strictly on faith and with a sense of fun, having nothing by which to prove — or disprove — any of it.

And as a matter of fact, there *was* a ghostly throng hanging out at the Consolidated Mine. They just weren't down in the tunnels.

Beside the concrete walkway to the gift shop was a raised section of landscaping about three feet high, with patio chairs and planted with pansies, Asiatic lilies, and greenery, which Brian remarked was a favorite garden spot for ghosts! "They love these stones, the gold in the mines, the flowers — all the *energy* here. They're in these chairs, sitting around."

"Oh come on, Brian. You mean they're just hanging out?"

"Earth is a beautiful place," he said. "They love to come back and visit. And once you're free of this thing" — he pointed at his body — "you can really appreciate it."

The astral plane, he explained, existed at a height several feet above the ground, which was why we often report seeing ghosts or angels hovering in mid-air. It's like looking into a raised window display at a department store.

Above the astral plane, said Brian, was Heaven — or a place that accorded with our individual ideas about Heaven.

"But why are these planes up high like that?"

"Because they exist at a higher vibration. That's why when you meditate you're actually projecting your consciousness, your light body, out of the physical form it thinks it's locked in, into a space above your physical body. That's why spirits and angels always look like they're dropping down." He took a deep breath. "Smell those wonderful lilies!"

"I think that's the pansies."

"And that *color*. See, that's the color of spirit."

"Spirit is *purple*?"

"The vibration of spirit is purple — or violet. That's the

color of the chakra where spiritual connection takes place." He paused and looked around. "The area around this mine is really arranged beautifully, much like the spirit realm. No wonder they love it here!"

Eagle Hotel building, known as the Besser Hotel in this photo

outwalking the emptiness

For he shall give his angels charge over thee, to keep thee in all thy ways. They shall bear thee up in their hands, lest thou dash thy foot against a stone.

— Psalms 91: 11-12

Two buildings standing side by side on the east side of the Square were erected in the 1940s by Henry Moore on the site originally occupied by the Eagle Hotel. The hotel was an enormous structure built a century earlier by General Harrison W. Riley, a name that often causes the raising of eyebrows and shaking of heads around Dahlonega.

Glenn Connor describes Riley as having had "a lot of shootouts out here in the Square. He was in the state legislature, but he was a desperado!" Andrew Cain writes in his 1932 *History of Lumpkin County* that General Riley "died a wealthy man, owning more real estate and money than any other man in this part of Georgia," but describes his career as long, stormy, and "picturesque." Local historian Anne Amerson quips that Riley mined the miners instead of the gold. The epigraph on his tombstone is almost an indictment: "Let his faults," it reads, "be buried with his bones."

With six dormers, the Eagle Hotel covered half the block. In the 1920s, it served as North Georgia College's only dormitory for women. Known by many names over its long history — including the Riley Hotel, the Besser Hotel, and the Wigwam — the place burned down in 1943.

Tommy Cobb is an amateur gold historian, a tough veteran with inexhaustible physical and intellectual energy. He once had a clock shop in the Moore building that now houses Golden Classics, where the south half of the Eagle Hotel once stood.

"I would be working downstairs at night — you couldn't get anything done during the day — and I would hear noises and footsteps," he told me one day while we were having lunch. "And this went on for quite a while. We had other merchants upstairs and I'd think one of them was up there, see? But actually I pooh-poohed a lot of it until I saw it."

"You *saw* the ghost?"

"Oh yes! She wanders the upstairs hall. She paces back and forth and she's constantly mumbling to herself and wiping her hands in her apron, like a tic or a fidget. And after this had been going on for a while, Deni [Tommy's wife] and I started watching for it. I had a huge antique table in the middle of the room, with six chairs, and every night we would push the chairs just so-so. Every morning we would come in, we'd look through the window. The chair at one end of the table would be turned out sideways. And I mean just numerous little oddities! I have seen her three or four different times walking the halls, in that stereotypical, foggy-looking, translucent —"

"How old would you say she was, Tommy?"

"Young. Early twenties."

"Did she ever tell you her name?"

"No! Never says anything! Just is constantly walking along mumbling to herself and wiping her hands in her apron. I've seen her upstairs and down — in the whole building, you know, in what would have been the old hotel. Now me with my embellishments and grandiose — I don't have —"

"You don't have any credibility, do you!" I said, laughing.

"No! That's the reason I say Deni is my best foil, so to speak. She's more grounded in the real than I am because I am theatrical, dramatic, and all that, see. But I just went through the third grade!"

I couldn't tell if Tommy was kidding about third grade. He was always talking in exclamations. I did know he'd had some hellacious Vietnam experiences (he'd told me so himself) and I'd bounced around in his jeep with him the day he and Jesse Rustin took me snooping around in old gold mines. I heard the entire gold history of the United States in four hours. It was like boot camp. I dragged around for two days afterward, just recovering from all that drama.

"But honestly now, Tommy. Do you have a history of being able to sense this sort of thing?"

"Well . . . we don't want to open a whole can of beans —"

"But it's important for me to know."

"— but this is my fourth life!"

"Ah, okay."

"You with me?"

"Only your fourth? That's not so good, Tommy!"

"Of what I can recall, see!" He grinned. "But this is the

only apparition I've ever seen and it was over a period of time."

Tommy said he never had a sense the woman was trying to communicate any information, but just seemed worried and self-absorbed. At one time, when he had over a hundred clocks in the store, he would come in some mornings to find that six or eight of them had stopped at exactly the same time, although the hour varied.

Bill Kinsland had some peculiar experiences, too, when his Hometown Book Store was in the basement of the building where the General Store is now and where the other half of the Eagle Hotel had stood. "I had the store on the left side there if you're coming up from the Smith House," Bill said, "and I had it all the way back to the front corner. And from that front corner sometimes in the evenings, before I'd close up, I'd hear a kind of shuffling and a moan. It was coming from that corner."

"And it always came from the same place?" I asked him.

"South Chestatee Street where it comes up from the Square, that corner. And I'd go over there to it, and it would continue off and on for maybe four or five minutes. It was mostly in the evenings, around six. Sometimes you wouldn't hear it for weeks, and then all of a sudden it would be back again. And I couldn't come up with any rational explanation in terms of a physical cause."

"Did you have a sense of a woman or a man?"

"I didn't have a sense of gender at all. It was just a deep, low-frequency moan."

"Like somebody in pain?"

"I got that feeling. And I had the sense of a presence. I could feel it. I don't know how else to put it."

Unlike Tommy, Bill never saw an apparition, but he did have problems keeping books on the shelves. "It wasn't like they were leaning or the shelf was unstable, but you would

Antique figures in the Moore building, where "Alissa" wanders

walk toward the back of the store and all of a sudden a book would fall out onto the floor."

"You'd hear it?"

"I'd *see* it. It would fall right off the shelf and — *boom!* — hit the floor. It startled the daylights out of me, and I couldn't *see* any visible cause for it. It happened two times I can actually remember. Different book each time, but the same shelf. It was against the inside wall — against the hallway wall, so to speak."

"Was that near where you heard the moaning?"

"No, that was on the opposite side and in the corner."

The Psychic Scoop

It was late and dark when Brian and I stood looking through plate glass windows into the basement of the building where Tommy Cobbs' clock shop had once been. Now, hundreds of antique toys, puppets, and life-size carnival figures were scattered in chaotic profusion through the room, and they cast an eerie quality over the place, as though time had stopped and caught them in mid-pose.

I had told Brian that a woman had been seen wandering the halls here, but I'd given him few details, so it surprised me to see him clutch his hands together at his stomach as he began telling me what he was "seeing" in his mind's eye.

"I feel this woman's name is Elizabeth, Eliza, Alissa, something like that," he said. "All I pick up from her is incredible sadness. Heaviness. Loss. Depression. It's awful."

"How old is she?"

"No older than 31, no younger than 26 or 27. She's a mature woman, but she's still very young. She just moves from one place to the other. It's like she's run this loop so long it's automatic."

"What time period is she from?"

"She's dressed like June Cleaver, so I'd say the Fifties, maybe early Sixties. The clothes are what I'm looking at because I can't get anything from her. There is this terrible sense of loss. This woman just wanders. Doesn't ask anything. I feel that she's looking for a baby she's lost and she's never come to terms with it, and she's just constantly walking, searching for that baby, hoping to outwalk the emptiness. That's why she never quits moving."

"Why is she in this building?"

"She's drawn here," Brian said. "Could be a lot of reasons."

"Is she conscious?"

"She's conscious, but she's locked in whatever the last loop of her life was. You can't communicate with her."

In Alissa's case, all we could do, said Brian, was ask that angels come and work with her in the hope that over time she would be able to see that there was another path, a light. Until that time, all the places she haunted would feel dark and sad.

Home to Wylie's Restaurant and the mischievous "Abby"

"Known for her hair"

Glenn Connor built the Connor Storehouse, which houses Wylie's Restaurant, in 1993 to accord architecturally with the old Jones home next door, which Glenn restored. Cool and atmospheric, Wylie's downstairs bar has an invisible resident who likes to tease the staff.

It was a Sunday and cold outside, but no matter how hard the air conditioner ran, the restaurant had been stifling all night long. Audrey Boynton, who tends bar and waits tables, had been running up and down the stairs to get wine and beer, and she was tired and ready to get home. She was helping close up and had gone downstairs to pick up some of her belongings when a black umbrella hanging on a coat peg near the steps started swinging out and back, out and back. She didn't waste any time getting out of there!

Erin Riley, the bartender, in the bar by herself one slow night, had rearranged the chairs at one of the tables and gone into the back room. When she returned, the chairs were back in their original positions. This puzzled her, but Erin doesn't ruffle easily. She rearranged the chairs a second time and went upstairs to get something. When she came back down after a few minutes, the chairs had moved again. "There was not a living soul down here but me," she said.

She was in the bar alone again one night when the bathroom door swung open and just stayed open. That door has a pneumatic hinge, so it's a struggle to open in the first place, and a race to keep it from hitting you in the behind when you let the doorknob go. No draft on earth can make it open by itself.

I loved these stories. They thrilled me.

"It's not so thrilling when you're down here by yourself!" said Erin, laughing.

The Psychic Scoop

I took Brian down to Wylie's bar before the after-work crowd arrived. He headed straight for the chair at the corner of the bar. "That's Glenn's chair," I said.

"There's somebody else here, too," Brian said. He paused. "She's very strong."

This peeved me to no end. "Then how come I can't see anything?" I huffed. I squinted at the chair, trying my best to "see" someone sitting there. Nothing.

Brian shook his head at me, clearly amused, then put his hand on the back of the chair and went on. "This woman's name is Ann, Abby — something like that," he said. "I

Abby's chair at Wylie's bar

believe she lived on the Square a long time ago, before they started tearing the houses down. I believe she wanders between this place and the house next door. That's where she comes from."

"What's she doing down here?"

Brian shrugged. "She likes watching people. This woman is very mischievous. She loves to play pranks. If people get scared, she picks on them. She goes upstairs and walks around, opens the doors. She says there's a lot of stuff she does but people don't notice it because they're so busy."

"Can you tell what she looked like?"

"Oh, she's very beautiful. She's not a thin woman, but she's not heavy. She was known for her hair. It was beautiful. Sable, almost like Indian hair, but softer. She always wore it down, even though it wasn't the fashion. She was a very active person. She loved to talk to people."

"How old is she?"

Brian paused. "I don't feel she ever married. She's like an old-maid aunt. No kids, no husband." Brian laughed. "She's really great. She says she was very outspoken, did a lot of things most women wouldn't do — rode horses through the Square, smoked — loved smoking. She was very flirtatious. But people said she was hard. Brash. She was really ahead of her time."

"How did she die?"

"She died in her sleep. I feel she was 84 when she died. It was fine with her. She knew she was dead. People might not have seen her any more, but she could still see them. She thought that was fun."

"But she doesn't want to leave?"

"It's not mandatory. She can leave any time she wants. She's happy."

"So she's here to stay?"

"For now." Brian paused. "She says thanks for talking to her. People should speak to her when they come in here," he said. "She likes that."

Building where Fred died under suspicious circumstances

suicide or murder?

"I had an uncle shot up here in '73," said Glenn Connor, cutting into a steak at Wylie's bar. "Fred Jones was my uncle."

Erin Riley, tending bar, handed me a glass of cabernet. She'd seen me so often lately I didn't even have to ask her for it. I was always in there telling my newest tales, interrogating the customers. Now I was asking Glenn about Fred Jones. Ever since I'd moved to Dahlonega I'd been hearing about this colorful character of a mayor and state legislator, who had died under suspicious circumstances in his Chevrolet dealership on the Square. Had it been suicide or murder? That was the mystery. The "official" story was suicide.

What was once Fred Jones's Chevrolet dealership is now

four stores and a café divided by a center hall, and the rumor that Fred haunts his building has been circulating for years. A waitress at the café — Dante's — told me a shadowy figure had often been seen sitting at a table by the front window of the restaurant, where Fred's office used to be. Others said they'd had "feelings" or seen someone walking down the hall at night. One woman who claimed to be "sensitive" told me she couldn't stand to go anywhere near the building and broke into tears while she was talking about it. "Something terrible happened in there," she said, but she couldn't be specific.

Now I was eager to hear Glenn's story of Fred's demise. "So was it murder or suicide?" I said. "What happened?"

Glenn said that one early August morning his aunt phoned him. "Something's happened to Fred down at the Chevrolet building!" she cried.

Glenn pulled on a pair of jeans and his loafers and hurried off to the dealership, but he couldn't get in the front door for all the curious people standing around outside. He ran around the block to the back of the building and came tearing into the dark service bay when a deputy yelled, "Look out! Look out!" Glenn glanced down just in time to leap over Fred's body, which was sprawled on the floor, a pistol close by.

I was rapt. "You think he was into something shady?" I said.

"There was a lot of gambling going on in those days," said Glenn. "I remember from when I was a kid."

Gambling was so prevalent around town that even the dealership was a venue for a lunch-time wager in a game involving a vending machine, a map of the United States, and strings tied to the necks of Coke bottles. I never could quite get the picture of how that worked.

"And I'd seen Fred go into these other little places around town and deal out cards," Glenn said, "throwing money down . . . and I don't know, but I've been told that the murder was trouble about the gambling."

"You think Fred stiffed somebody?"

"I think he got in an argument over a gambling debt, and I think he probably pulled out a pistol and they got to fighting over it and it just happened. I think it was an accident, but I think that's how it happened. But Fred was a real nice guy. A real, real nice guy."

The Psychic Scoop

The next time Brian came to town, I took him to the Fred Jones building and told him the jury was still out (at least in the local imagination) about what had really happened to Fred. It seemed he was still around, making his presence known. I pointed out the café windows and led him down the dim hall, vaguely wishing that a ghostly form would see us and come floating out to talk.

At the end of the hall, I pointed to the space inside Dean's jewelry store, where Glenn had jumped over Fred's body. "Are you getting anything?" I asked Brian, spooked by my own imaginings: poor Fred lying there on the concrete, blood pooling around his body, pistol a few feet away, GBI agents hovering. "Can you see what happened?"

"Oh, he was murdered," said Brian authoritatively. "He was murdered by two men he had a really bad connection with."

Only Brian couldn't say exactly what sort of connection that was.

Whatever the nature of the three men's relationship, Brian explained that their last exchange drove the terror surrounding the final moments of Fred's life up to such a pitch that it left a psychic imprint, a kind of vibratory residue that remained present in the environment. The agates and crystals Dean kept on display in his jewelry store only intensified the vibration.

"This man was doing some serious begging toward the end," said Brian.

Homer Head house, where Rick's Restaurant is a haven for ghosts

Aunt Nine
and the stay behinds

"Stay behinds" are relatively common. Somebody dies, and then they're really surprised that all of a sudden they [don't feel] dead. They're alive like they were. They don't understand it because they weren't prepared for it. So they go back to what they knew most — their chair, their room — and they just sit there. Next, they want to let people know they're still "alive." So they'll do little things like moving things, appear to relatives, pushing objects — poltergeist phenomena, and so on.
— Dr. Hans Holzer,
2005 interview with Jeff Belanger

In 1908, Dr. Homer Head paid $53.11 for the lumber in the nearby Baptist Church being torn down to make way for a new church building and built his large home on Park Street, a block east of the Square. In 1909 he married Nina McClure. Known fondly as "Aunt Nine," she loved children and was herself a skilled healer, having learned some of the healing arts from her husband. She had just turned ninety when she died in 1975 a few days after a stroke she suffered as she was about to have lunch at a restaurant in town.

For seven years, Rick Whorf has run Rick's Restaurant out of the old Head home, and he's had all kinds of ghosts flitting around. Erin Riley saw the water in the dish room sink come on by itself. She actually watched the handle turn! The servers often feel someone following them down the first-floor hallway or sense a hand on a shoulder.

The radio turns itself on and off and changes its channels, the toilet flushes when no one is in the bathroom, and a chef who once lived in the attic apartment was scared out of his wits one night when he awoke with the feeling that someone was pressing him down in his bed. He cleared out fast after that.

I hung around at Rick's a lot, hoping to see the toilet flush itself or a shadowy form sitting at my table, but nothing ever happened.

Now clad in his apron with his sleeves rolled up, Rick leaned in the kitchen doorway drinking beer while I plied him with questions. He's a curly-haired, cheerful guy with an open mind, a fun sense of humor, and an "up east" accent.

Just that day, Rick was saying, one of his servers was so sure she'd seen another server in the hall that she followed her into the kitchen. But no one was there.

"It's like when you have a mouse in your house," said Rick. "You know you just saw him, but he's gone. I was frying potato chips one morning when I saw something out of the corner of my eye. When I looked over at it, it had disappeared. But I could remember it. It was a small boy, curly hair like my son Nathan got, right? But he was a little bigger, had on a white shirt, suspenders, blue shorts, high socks with garters, and black shiny shoes. That was the most impressive thing I've experienced. The feelings and electrical stuff, I don't know."

Like so many people who have told me stories, Rick had a history. At a Virginia cabin he lived in, he awoke one morning to find all the strings on his bamboo shades pulled out and hung on the backs of chairs. Another morning after a heavy thunderstorm he found all his dresser drawers stacked in front of the dresser.

"That's so *eerie!*" I said. "There's a ghost on the Square that lines up chess pieces down the middle of the chessboard. Why don't things like that happen to *me*?"

Rick said that on separate occasions two psychics had told him the Head home was full of spirits. A ghost boy played on the swing in the yard, a woman and child ran to the front door when guests came in, and a tall, dark figure stood behind people. He wasn't bad or evil, said Rick, just there.

Aunt Nine Leaves A Message

I kept insisting I wasn't sensitive to paranormal phenomena. My trouble was, if I felt a sudden chill or got goose bumps or thought I heard something, I'd talk myself into thinking I'd imagined it. I wanted something *big* to happen, something I couldn't argue with. I wanted a saltshaker to fly off a table. "I want to *know*," I kept telling Chase.

Then one night I was having supper at Rick's with Bogy Patton and my mother, who had come up from South

Georgia to visit. While Bogy and Mom were talking, I saw a flash of light near the ceiling. At that moment, through the window I glimpsed a man walking by about three feet off the ground. He was only visible from the waist up, and even that was in profile, but the afterimage was clear. He was tall, slender, dark-haired but graying, perhaps in his early fifties. It happened so fast, I wasn't sure I saw him. Then I remembered Rick's analogy: it was as though I'd seen a mouse scamper by and turned to look . . . but he was gone.

Chase and I spent many an evening on the various floors at Rick's, trying to record EVP. The first half-dozen tries, we were unsuccessful. I spent hours listening with headphones to long, frustrating silences in response to the questions I would pose (always feeling ridiculous) to the ether. "Is anyone here?" Pause. "Can we help you?" Pause. "Can you say your name?" Pause. And so on and so forth *ad nauseum*.

Then one night I saw something.

I'd been doing research on the Head house and its original occupants, and even though Brian had assured me I had nothing to fear from ghosts, I was always scared when Chase and I climbed the ladder into the dark attic. There was no light but for a few small windows and a blacklight that, in keeping with the electrical anomalies in the house, sometimes flickered briefly.

We'd been up there a long time one night, recording, when I saw the word *HELLO* forming on the wall! The O was fading, but it was there.

"Oh, my Lord. Chase! Do you see that?" I said, pointing. I was scared to death but ecstatic. "Great! That's just great!" I kept saying. "Thank you! That's just great! H-E-L-L-O! Chase, do you see it?"

"Are you sure that's not H-E-L-L?" Chase said. "It looks like HELL to me. Where's the O?"

"Right there! Anyway it can't be HELL! Who are you?" I

practically yelled. "Can you say your name?"

We sat in thrilled silence a while, looking at the "sign" on the wall and nudging each other, and I asked a few more questions for the recorder, although frankly I half expected one of the dishes from the pile behind us to take flight and sail across the room.

And then something caught my eye, and I glanced at the ceiling . . . saw a cluster of pale stars . . . and a big *HI!* . . . and realized, in utter embarrassment, that the chef or some other attic tenant had gone around with a fluorescent marker writing messages on the walls! Somehow Chase and I had failed to notice these "signs" before. I felt more ridiculous than ever, and we gave up for the night.

But I couldn't argue with hard evidence.

It wasn't long before we went back for another try. Ten minutes into the session, I asked, very slowly: "Can you say your name?"

And faintly, just loud enough for me to make it out, came a response. It was pitched exactly as my voice was pitched, but with a kind of singing quality: "Aunt Nine."

A few nights later we were having supper at Rick's before going upstairs to try for something more definitive. "Okay, Aunt Nine," I whispered, "if that was really you, you're going to have to be louder or something because I can barely hear you. If that was really you, I need some clearer answers."

Suddenly the light dimmed in our room, then in the adjacent room, then again in our room, and at that moment a waitress I'd never met — Ferris Brewer — suddenly pulled up a chair, sat down, and said: "So you want to hear about Aunt Nine?"

Chase and I looked at each other.

"My grandfather is Hoyt Robinson," Ferris said. "He grew up in Gainesville, but he bought a lot of land here and got married and raised cattle on Long Branch Road. Well, he was always a big fan of Aunt Nine, and Aunt Nine was a big fan of him, too: they were real good friends. Her name was not Nine, it was something else."

"It was Nina," I said, reeling from this burst of information.

"Nina. She used to own a farm on the Etowah River that had been passed down through generations, and when the nursing home, Gold City, got built, he came by here and asked her if she had gone to see it, hinting around that maybe it was time for her to go, too. She said, 'No, I want to stay here. I go to see my friends over there now and then, and every time, they turn down the bedsheets for me.'

"She used to come buy cows from him whenever one of hers would die, and she'd drive her old long Cadillac, and every time she came to get a cow she'd say, 'All right, I want you to put it in a sack so it won't mess up the back of my car.' And she'd take that cow home in the trunk of her car.

"And he said she was one of the best ladies he's ever met, that she took care of a lot of kids, and that she would get a twinkle in her eye when she talked to you.

"He told me all those stories today at lunch. He said if you ever want to know anything more about Aunt Nine, just let him know."

I couldn't help it. Ferris's appearance at our table was so unexpected, and her timing in response to my whispered entreaty was so exquisite, that I took the whole experience as confirmation that the voice I had heard on my recorder really was Aunt Nine's.

The Psychic Scoop (and I Hear a Ghost)

Now, even though I liked Brian immensely and believed *he* believed in his work, and despite capturing the voice of (ostensibly) Aunt Nine on my recorder, I felt silly talking to ghosts as if they were my next-door neighbors. I just wasn't

Attic stairs to Aunt Nine

sure any of this was any more "real" than what happened when creative people with giant-sized imaginations got addicted to excitement. It was going to take something *really* huge — my dresser drawers to stack themselves up on the floor — to convince me.

At supper the night we were preparing to "read" at Rick's I told Brian all this. He said that Native American tradition called for me to offer tobacco to the spirits and ask them to show themselves to me. So I did, around the corner of the house under the kitchen window. Quietly, while hiding behind a tree.

Still, I had done enough work with Indians in years past to understand that my tobacco offering was considered sacred and, like smoke in many traditions, believed to carry my prayer into the spiritual realm, even to God. So who knew what would happen? For despite my self-consciousness about the work I was doing, I was sincere.

It wasn't long before we climbed the ladder to Rick's attic. Brian took some deep breaths, preparing to find out who was around. We were standing near a half-dozen steps piled with dishes, which led to a landing six feet off the floor where an old mattress leaned against the wall behind two straight chairs.

"That's where they are," said Brian, nodding at the landing. "Up there."

"Well, what about that dark space over there behind the curtain? Or that crawl space?" Both were appropriately dark and spooky, I thought.

Brian shook his head. "Two ladies are here."

"Are they. Hey," I said to the ladies, that being the customary greeting (rather than "hi") in Georgia.

"One is called Anna, I believe. She wants to speak to you."

"Could it be Aunt Nine?" I said. (The first time I heard Aunt Nine's voice on my recorder, I'd thought she was saying Anna.)

"She says she's been here a long time and she's really tired, keeping these others company. She feels so burdened down. She says she'd leave except she doesn't want to abandon this fellow here."

"What fellow?"

Brian glanced at me. "You're looking right at the chair where she's sitting. You're doing great."

"I don't see a soul," I said peevishly. "What fellow, Brian?"

Brian turned toward the middle of the room and began walking in that direction, then put his hand out. He seemed to be listening for something. Suddenly he put his hand to his chest and sighed. "This fellow — this is the one she's staying with. I feel he was born William, but he was called Billy. Also Junior. I believe this man died of a heart attack — was this woman's husband a doctor?"

"Yes. He built this house."

Brian took a breath. "I feel this man died of a heart attack here around his early forties. Early 1900s. He says he comes from the mountain J.B. Stone owns. He's in overalls, about five-ten. Has thick black hair. Aunt Nine's was the last face he saw, his last impression. He was terrified to die. He's terrified of going to hell. He's very confused. He's scared."

"Can you talk to him?"

"Yes. I'm going to tell him there's nothing to fear about going on," Brian said, walking toward the middle of the room. "I'm going to tell him there's no danger, nothing bad waiting." Brian paused. "He can't quite figure this out."

"It doesn't make sense to him," I ventured. "Given what he was probably taught about hell. I mean if he's that scared of it."

"He says he doesn't want anybody up here. He tried to run somebody out of here. He's showing me a picture of bending over somebody, doing this." Brian was imitating pushing down on someone from above.

I had not told him about the chef being pressed down in the bed. "He *did* do that. How come?"

"Because this is all frightening to him. He doesn't know what's going on. He can talk, he's screaming, he's yelling, he's waving — people don't see him. Now I don't know if you can see it or not, Amy, but there's a white cloud coming in here. This whole area is filling up. Billy's coming into the room now. He's stepping out of that closet."

I couldn't see a thing.

"The relief!" Brian said. "It's beginning to fill the air here. Billy says he feels better now. He's so glad to have someone to talk to. He says he never married, never had time for it. Now, though, he's had a lot of time to think."

"I'll bet," I said. I didn't know what to think. All these ghosts around and I without any sense of a presence? Could I be that insensitive?

"He's still a little uncertain, but he says that if Aunt Nine will go with him, he thinks he'd like to leave now."

"Well," I said. "That's good."

Brian explained to Billy that if he would turn around, he would see his family coming to greet him. Aunt Nine was (according to Brian) relieved to be able to leave at last. Brian conducted one of his elaborate ceremonies and asked the spirits to acknowledge that they wanted to leave. Then he blessed them, and with Aunt Nine beside him, Billy crossed over to the Other Side.

I felt no change in the room, but as I was watching Brian orchestrate all this, I saw something strange. "Brian," I said. "I can see light."

"Can you see the cloud?"

"I don't see a cloud, I just have a sense of light. A kind of mistiness."

"You're actually seeing etheric energy."

"Is that right?"

"The spirits heard you downstairs. You said you wanted to see something."

"I *can* see. It's very vague, though. It's formless, white, sort of misty energy. It's just hanging there in the middle of the room."

The mistiness didn't really scare me; it wasn't threatening enough to be scary. I just thought it was strange. It stayed there while Brian spoke with four other spirits. The detail with which he described these entities surprised me, so I asked him what he actually saw when he "saw" ghosts.

"They have a solid-looking appearance, but you can tell they're really not solid."

"Are they transparent?"

"It's more of an ethereal quality. What happens to me is that I sense someone coming toward me, and when I turn my mind toward that person, I get an image. When the image comes in close, it's like it clicks with my eyes, and I can project what is in my mind out to where they're actually standing."

"And these people have gender? I don't get that."

"People always have a favored gender, and they return to it on the Other Side. When they're coming to communicate with a loved one, they usually appear the way that loved one knew them. But everybody holds a gender. There is no androgyny — well, not at that level of consciousness."

Brian talked to Sarah, a polite 12-year-old from *my family* who was keeping me company. She stayed at my left side. She wore a dress from the early 1900s and had freckles and long dark hair, which she pulled back with a wide band. She had my bone structure, Brian said.

Ida Mae was the widow of one of the founders of the original Baptist Church, whose timbers had been used to build the Head home. For Ida, the house represented her connection to her husband. For the present, she was content to stay in the house and wanted Rick to know that she thought he was a very good cook. She often visited him in the kitchen, she said. She was happy for people to visit her, as long as they understood the building was a church and they showed respect.

Timothy was a young boy who had died of polio and was now loving being able to run and play. He was an active spirit, the one who had been seen in the yard. He loved the cat who hung around the house. He, too, was not interested in leaving. He was the boy Rick had seen in the kitchen.

I had been following Brian around with my recorder during this long session, while he spoke to the ghosts and relayed their stories to me. Now my energy was flagging — in fact, I was exhausted — and I was about to suggest we wrap things up, when suddenly I heard sounds across the room, as though someone were moving among the boxes stored there. There was an irregular clicking, like tapping, along the wall. "What's that noise, Brian?" I said, spooked.

He turned and began to approach the sound, but stopped. "That's somebody we haven't spoken to yet," he said, the caution plain in his voice. "He doesn't want to be ignored. Now, that's not very nice of you!" Brian said to the spirit.

"Is it a she or a he?" I said, alarmed. I was still hearing the ticking sound, but nothing was *there*. I'd never seen Brian being cautious and that was unnerving.

"It's a he."

"What's he doing?"

"He's hoping to scare us."

"Well, he's doing a pretty good job."

Brian knelt down and slowly extended his hand. After a moment, he said, "Amy, this man has not been dead long."

"That gives me the creeps, Brian."

"He's just terrified."

"What does he need from us?"

"Let me get past his fear first. I'm going to tell him we're not here to force anything, that if he wants us to, we'll leave him alone." He paused, then said, "I'm explaining that Billy and Aunt Nine wanted to leave." Pause. "I'm picking up that this is a young man, 30 to 32. He died in a motorcycle wreck."

"That's horrible."

"He's very upset."

"When you say he hasn't been dead long, do you mean twenty or thirty years?"

"I mean months."

"Ooooo!" The thought of someone recently dead really spooked me.

"This man died around here in the last six to nine months. He has this terrible guilt. He says he wasn't paying attention.

He had a wife and child — he's worried about them. He was Catholic. He's scared to death. He's afraid he committed suicide because of the way this happened."

"Can you tell him that God understands? That God still loves him?" At least that's what I believed.

"You can't do anything in this place right here," Brian said to the man. "This isn't some trick. I'm not an exorcist; you're not a demon. If you will go to the light, there will be no more of this. If you want to come back, you're free to do so. But I don't think that once you get there you'll want to come back." He paused. "Those people are there to help you." Pause. "Go in peace."

Then Brian fell silent. At last he took a deep breath, looked over at me, and said: "I can breathe now."

And at that moment, I felt something like a whisper at my left side and then a deep surge of well-being. "Brian," I said, "I just got major goose bumps."

"He went by you."

"He did?"

"He was thanking you."

This humbled me, although I still wasn't sure what I believed about what was happening. When it came right down to it, I just tried to remind myself, with nothing to tell me otherwise, that I should take all of it on faith. What was the harm? If these people really did exist in the in-between, then we were helping them. If they didn't, then we were certainly doing no harm. And I left Rick's that night with a tremendous admiration for Brian's devotion to the controversial cause he was championing, his courage in the face of the incredible skepticism the world harbored for things of this nature, and his clear love for all us souls struggling to satisfy our human longing to reach the divine.

Hall building, where "Martha" moves things around

the chessboard ghost

You know these five physical senses were not made to contact spirit; they were made for us to live and operate on the physical plane. When people want something physical to convince them of the spiritual, they're asking for something that's virtually impossible. So you have to learn — and this is what meditation does — that you are more than this body. Because you are not just this body. That is the illusion.

— Brian Keith
in a conversation with the author

The building whose second floor now houses Gabee's Cajun Kitchen and the ArtCart was built by Captain Frank Hall in 1881 as a personal residence and boarding house — and I quickly discovered that the place had its share of ghostly tenants who were making their presence known. Invisible dishes shattered in the kitchen, footsteps echoed in the art studio, doors unlocked themselves, and chess pieces moved around in the middle of the night!

Mike and Helen Miller's ArtCart is both art studio and store, and it is Mike's habit to sit on a stool behind a counter at the back of the store, facing the foyer so he can greet people when they come in.

Because Mike is so often occupied with his painting, he has developed an ear for the sound of footsteps. Especially when the store is quiet, he can hear someone walking through the foyer to stand beside the heater in front of the counter: the boards creak. But when he looks up to greet his customer, no one is there. The sound is so distinct that sometimes he wonders whether the person has already wandered into the next room. But no one ever comes out.

Mike has a handful of ceramic figures, little men holding "wet paint" signs that warn customers away from newly painted art. From time to time, he finds one of them broken on the floor.

One cold, rainy February morning while Mike was chatting with his son Patrick and the Mikels, who own Gabee's across the hall, he spied one of the little men on the floor under a cabinet. It had lost an arm. Mike glued the figure back together and set it beside a caricature of Pee-Wee Herman he kept on the counter.

After a while, Charles Mikel left to stir his pots in the restaurant kitchen and found that the little man had somehow moved all the way from Mike's counter in the ArtCart to a shelf in the hall beside the kitchen door.

On another day, while Mike was making coffee in the ArtCart one morning he found that a fabric bag that held tissues had moved itself from the top corner of a top shelf to the floor on the opposite side of the room. There were no bits of tissue around, no evidence of mice. It was a small thing, but it bothered Mike. He couldn't see any reason for it.

Once Mike found two stools moved to opposite ends of the room.

Then there was the time Mike's mother, visiting the store, looked at her son curiously and said, "What are we going to do about all these people coming through the window?"

When Mike asked her what people, she said, "All these ladies in long dresses and these men in uniform. Oh! It's too late," she said, disappointed. "They've gone out the door."

Gabee's, too, has its unsolved mysteries. It isn't unusual for people to hear dishes crashing in the kitchen or heavy objects being dropped in the front room . . . only when someone rushes in to see what's happening, nothing is there.

But this was the mystery that most puzzled me. Mike had painted a chessboard on the surface of an old wooden coffee table. He fashioned the chess pieces from gourds and painted them to look like Muslims and Christians. One day while he was working at the counter, he glanced at the chessboard. . . and found the chess pieces lined up down the middle of the board! A few weeks later, he found them lined up *around the edge of the coffee table*. Sometimes, if he leaves for the night with the pieces set as though a game is in progress, he finds them returned to their home positions the next morning.

As if this weren't weird enough, Charles once found his tennis shoes turned on their sides and *stacked on top of each other!* Like Rick's stacked dresser drawers, I found this phenomenon particularly disturbing — perhaps because it seemed so *deliberate*.

The Psychic Scoop

I took Brian up to the balcony at Gabee's for a reading. He asked for water. I asked for wine.

"Hey. A pot moved today," Charles told me when he brought the drinks.

"You're kidding. Really? Did you see it move?"

"Nope. Put it down one place, turn 'round, go back, pot sittin' in another place." Charles is Cajun and he strings his sentences together like that.

I was instantly envious. "Why don't things happen to me?" I complained to Brian.

He just looked tickled. "Things have happened to you."

"But I mean big things."

"Why is that so important to you?"

"Because then I'd *know* something."

"Don't you know something now?"

I shook my head, exasperated, and drank my wine. Presently, I said: "Who moves the chess pieces around in this house?"

"That's a woman," said Brian. "She's agitated because she's been trying to get someone's attention for a long time, and now it's turned into a game. Her name is Martha Jennings, Martha James — maybe Martha Jane. She says she's keeping the woman downstairs company. That's why she's still here."

"There's a woman downstairs, too?"

"There's a woman downstairs by the front door. She's trapped here. She seems to be locked in some deep grief. She just died recently. She's afraid the man in the store down there is not going to be okay without her. I'm going to tell her that he'll be okay."

"Was she kin to him?"

"She was his wife." Brian paused, then sighed. "Okay. There was a shift. I can breathe now."

"Does that mean Martha can leave?"

"She says she'll go on now, but she's afraid that Mike will miss her."

"Tell her not to worry about Mike. He's glad for her to go. We talked about it." I had told Mike that there was a chance he might lose his ghost, if my medium could help her. Curiously, Mike and Charles thought the spirit was male. I was certain the presence was female, though I couldn't say why.

"Martha has enjoyed being here," said Brian. "She's enjoyed looking out on the Square from the windows upstairs. Her death was a hard one. They were taking her to the hospital, passing through the Square, and she didn't make it. She died of a heart attack about five years ago."

"What about the man who died in this building? People say there was a man."

Brian fell quiet, then shook his head. "Not in this building. There is another woman here, though. She's very heavyset."

"Not a man?"

"Not unless he was so out of shape and huge that he looked like a woman. Because the image I pick up is of somebody who is grossly overweight. But she's not responsible for the noise — the dishes falling and all that. That was Martha. She wanted somebody to *hear* her."

We left soon after that. I never asked Brian about the dressed up men and women that Mike's mother saw. In fact, there were many little incidents he never commented about in our readings. But I thought it would be more fun to leave a few mysteries unsolved. And if any of those ghosts wanted help, I decided, they'd find a way to let me know.

McGuire House, where a ghostly hostess still keeps house

the McGuire House haunting

Built in 1882 by Goodman McGuire as his personal residence, this house a block west of the Square has been a restaurant for some time. Jennifer Fogleman, a server for Renee's Restaurant before it was sold and became the current McGuire House restaurant, had some bizarre experiences in the last few months before Renee's closed. Jeff Weaver had already told me he'd seen a picture fall and felt cold spots on the second floor. Now Jennifer was telling me the staff would arrive some mornings to find the dining room chairs on their backs, the silverware moved around, and the mirrors slanted on the walls.

And on the second floor, she said, the temperature

sometimes dropped so dramatically that she stopped going upstairs to wash the linens. Instead, she asked her fiancée, executive chef Randy Davis, to do it for her.

But one night Randy went up to wash the linens and didn't come back down for a long time. When he finally did show up, he was pale as a sheet. And what a story he told. He had put the linens in the dryer, he said, and was on his way out of the room, when his leg hit a table and knocked off a pepper mill. He put it back, but as he turned to leave, he heard the pepper mill fall again. Perhaps he hadn't set it down firmly enough, he thought. So he placed it on the table a third time, against the wall. He was leaving the room at last when the pepper mill fell *again* . . . but this time it landed five feet away.

Bravely, Randy introduced himself. "I know you don't want the restaurant to close," he said, "and I know you're here. We're on your side. We won't let anything happen to the house."

Then suddenly, said Randy, the room turned ice-cold. This time without a backward glance Randy slammed the pepper mill down on the table and beat a hasty retreat downstairs to the safety of the restaurant.

The Psychic Scoop

It was the end of a long day of psychic work when Brian and I wrapped up our last reading at the McGuire house. As we stood on the porch, Brian explained that the ghost who inhabited the place was a sociable woman who had lived in the house and despised being by herself. While the restaurants were thriving, she loved to wander among the guests, playing the invisible hostess. When she learned that Renee's was going to close, she was terrified that she would be left alone, so she let the staff know she was unhappy by moving things around.

Now that the restaurant is busy again, she moves things around to let the staff know she's watching them. She's very particular about how the place is kept, said Brian. "That's still her house and she has no desire to leave it. If the staff finds something out of place, she's letting them know she's there. But there's nothing to be afraid of. She's happy as long as she has company."

Butler building, where ghostly children play

playful spirits in the Butler Building

In 1947 the Butler Building was erected on the site of the old Burnside Hotel, which burned in 1904. The Butler family lived upstairs and operated a furniture store and other businesses on the first floor. Now the building houses a handful of shops and a restaurant.

A woman who was once the proprietor of a shop on the first floor told me she had often heard the bell on a shop door ringing, but no one ever appeared. Sometimes she heard footsteps coming down the hall and the sound of her door opening and closing, but when she went to greet her customer, no one was there.

This ghost liked to move things around in the upstairs apartment, too. Visiting a friend who lived there, Erin Riley was pouring wine one night when she heard a sound behind her, turned, and saw the plates falling out of the kitchen cabinet one by one. When she approached the cabinet to try and stop them, the light fixture in the ceiling came crashing to the floor!

The Psychic Scoop

Brian and I were standing in the grass on the lower level of the Butler building when I told him about Erin and the plates. "She was pretty scared," I said, "and she's the sort of person who doesn't rattle easily."

Brian chuckled. "But there's nothing to be scared of," he said, looking up at the dark second-floor windows. "This is just children."

"You're kidding, Brian. Children?"

"There's a little girl who's the leader of the group, and they either lived together or for some reason spent a lot of time together upstairs. I don't know if there was an orphanage here at one time or why they were all together. But they have a playful, happy energy. They just like being here."

"But what about that light fixture? It just missed landing on Erin's head!"

"Well, it didn't, did it?"

"No, but —"

"Listen, Amy. These children love to make people aware of their presence. They like to ring that little bell, run down the hall. They're kids! They love Halloween and all the times, like during festivals, when the Square gets busy, because they like to walk around with all the tourists. They're happy here. They're not going anywhere . . . at least not for now."

Old bank, where "the Colonel" haunts Jack's Café

"the Colonel"
freezes Erin Peck in place

The ghost of "the Colonel" is a legend among Dahlonega merchants. Some believe he's the spirit of Colonel William Pierce Price, who founded the school now known as North Georgia College and State University and was instrumental in other aspects of Dahlonega and Georgia history throughout the latter half of the 1800s.

In any case, *somebody's* about, and he likes kitchens. He

gets around all over the Square, but seems to prefer the east side, especially Jack's Café in the old Bank of Dahlonega building. Dr. Homer Head built the place in the early 1900s and for a while had his medical office on the second floor. Now Jack and Erin Peck use the old bank vault for storage.

Jack's small kitchen has a large grill, and on it the Pecks keep a spatula and a boiler pan lid they use for covering hamburgers. Attached to the front of the grill is a long cutting board, and between the cutting board and the grill is a space a few inches wide. When "the Colonel" isn't getting enough attention, Erin Peck says, he pushes the boiler pan lid around on the grill — *tink!* The noise is loud enough to carry into the dining room. Once he tipped the lid up so that it slipped down between the cutting board and the front of the stove. When he's really in the mood to be acknowledged, he flips the spatula across the room!

"Have you ever seen these things while they were airborne?" I asked Erin, fascinated that a ghost was tossing pot lids and spatulas around. We were sitting at a table in the dining room drinking sweet tea while I listened to Erin tell ghost stories. It was mid-afternoon on a weekday, and the café was quiet.

"I've been standing at the condiment bar a few feet away and caught them out of the corner of my eye going down," said Erin. "Once when I was talking to somebody about selling the café, the spatula came down and hit me in the foot."

The Colonel doesn't like it when tensions run high, said Erin, and he doesn't care at all for loud rap music. Once when she was at the sink washing dishes, a car went by with a boom box blaring so loud the windows shook. All of a sudden the boiler lid sailed off the grill, went sliding across the floor, and almost hit Erin in the heels. "I don't like loud rap music either," she told the Colonel.

The servers have seen things, too. One young woman was so badly frightened when the dishes lifted off a shelf and crashed to the floor that she turned in her notice and fled.

But Erin believed the Colonel was harmless. "I think he just wants us to know he's there," she said.

It's pretty clear, though, that whoever this ghost is, he doesn't like to be challenged.

It was August and the night was hot the way Georgia late-summer nights can be — windless and so humid that just breathing can wear you out. Erin had stayed late to finish painting the café floor, and it was nearing eleven by the time she finally finished cleaning up. Mentally and physically exhausted, she kept seeing what looked like the figure of a man out of the corner of her eye. For an instant she thought it was Jack — but remembered he was at home with their boys. She was getting ready to turn out the lights and leave when it hit her: this was the Colonel. He was checking up on her. And she dismissed the experience . . . sort of. Because even though she didn't feel the Colonel was out to hurt anyone, he was still a *ghost*, after all.

As she came around the corner from the bathroom, the Colonel appeared again. He was standing on the opposite side of the swinging door to the kitchen, barely ten feet away. He was like a silhouette, said Erin. She could see no distinguishing features, and nothing about his clothing was clear, but he was six feet tall and most definitely *there*. She was tired and hot and hungry, and the apparition startled her so badly she got mad. "Don't *do* that, Colonel!" she yelled. "Don't be stupid!" She picked up her stuff and headed out fast. But six feet from the front door she was stopped dead in her tracks.

"I was dripping sweat, hot — nervous, too — and all of a sudden from my right shoulder I suddenly felt — starting from the right side of my body and melting through — this cold sensation. It wasn't like a breeze; it was from the tip of my head to the bottom of my toes, and it was working its way into me. *Cold.* I literally froze, in both senses of the word. I could *not* move. I just stood there, until it permeated my whole body. By then I was apologizing every way I could think of: 'Okay, Colonel. You're right. *I'm* the stupid one. I shouldn't have yelled at you. I'm sorry. I won't do that again. I should have known better,' just anything. And then the cold slowly started working its way out the left side of my body, just as gradually as it had come in from the right side, and I was paralyzed until the last ounce of it was gone from my left shoulder."

I gulped down some tea. "Then what happened?" I said. "Did you run?"

"I started dripping sweat. I went from hot to cold, from cold to hot, and then I could move again. And I said, very sweetly, 'I'm going home now, Colonel! See you later!' I got out of there."

Later, Erin thought the Colonel was angry with her, because for several weeks, he made himself . . . invisible. No pot lids *tinked* across the grill — at least not while Erin was around. Jack, however, wasn't getting the brush-off. He'd come home from the café reporting all kinds of friendly visits.

Erin had become fond of the Colonel, and this punishment grieved her. After a few weeks, she went to work one morning and made a formal apology for her harsh words. She asked the Colonel to forgive her and come back . . . and the spatula instantly fell to the floor. "Nice to see you again, Colonel!" she said. He's been nudging the boiler pan lid ever since.

Whitmire building, home of "the Colonel"

"the Colonel" —
in his own words

It was an April afternoon when Brian and I were nosing around in the Crimson Moon, a coffee house and performance venue for musicians and artists that operates out of the old Parker Storehouse. Built in 1858, the Storehouse is the oldest building on the Square except for the courthouse.

For months, I'd been hearing stories from the Crimson Moon staff about spices flying off the kitchen shelves, cold spots on the stairs, and dim, fleeting figures haunting the offices upstairs. Now I peeked into the dark closet under the steps and was instantly spooked, feeling like Fortunato in Poe's "The Cask of Amontillado," about to be chained up and walled in.

"This is all the Colonel," said Brian when I escorted him into the kitchen. "He's a little out of his element over here. I usually see him on the lower level of the Massachusetts Bay Trading Company."

That was the building next door to Jack's Café.

"Well, what's he been doing over here, then?"

"Let's go ask him," said Brian with a grin.

We made our way across the Square through swirls of noisy tourists in town for the Bear on the Square Mountain Music Festival.

The Massachusetts Bay Trading Company is in the building built by Wiley Americus Whitmire in 1935 to replace an older two-story frame structure. Now stocked with Native American jewelry, power objects, blankets, and pottery, the store was a calm, sage-scented refuge from the chaos outside.

Carol Edwards, the proprietor, had already told me how her front door mysteriously opened itself and things in the store moved around. Erin Peck had assured her the Colonel was only paying her visits. Apparently, Erin was right.

Brian and I walked down the few steps to the lower level at the back of the store. He took deep breaths and paced the large room while I poked around in the corners, whispering things like, "Hey, Colonel. You here?" and "We're coming to hang out at your place for a while." Joking around. Wondering whether I was about to have the wool pulled over my eyes in a big way.

A customer who got wind of what we were doing came and sat down on a bench to watch. Carol leaned over the railing. It was a regular séance, I thought. Maybe we should light a candle and hold hands.

"Colonel, you home?" said Brian, wandering around the room. Then suddenly he turned and grinned at me. "He says it's about time you got to him! He's glad to see you!"

I rolled my eyes. Sometimes it just seemed so implausible that Brian was actually in contact with a ghost. Nevertheless, I sighed and launched into the spirit of the thing. "Tell him it's good to see him, too — or not to see him."

That got a laugh.

"What's his story?" I said.

"His story is that he's not a colonel at all," said Brian.

"Well, that's going to upset some apple carts," I said.

"He thinks it's his job to keep things stirred up around here," said Brian. "He gets around!"

"Is that him that keeps moving things around in the kitchens?"

"He says that's where life takes place. He loves kitchens."

"Well, why did he freeze Erin Peck like that?"

"She was asking for a good scare, so he gave her one!"

"If he's not a colonel," said Carol, "then what is he?"

"He says he was a simple man. He worked in the bank on the corner. He owned some land on the other side of the Ridleys' place, went to church. People have always called him the Colonel, even while he was alive."

"Why?" I said.

"Because of how he carried himself," said Brian. "He was elegant and charming, especially with the ladies. When they started calling him 'Colonel,' he didn't see any reason not to let them keep the myth."

"Well, we're about to blow that all to bits," I said wryly.

"He says that's fine. You're the writer. He's not going anywhere. He likes it here."

"What does he look like?" said the customer, a bright-looking woman with a shrewd expression.

"He looks like a colonel ought to look," said Brian. "He's tall, has white hair. He's a big, good-looking man, likes being the center of attention. He's famous. He likes it that way." Brian stopped and threw Carol a sideways glance. "He thinks you're spunky. You remind him of his wife."

"Well, I want to see him!" said Carol.

"Don't we all," I said, rolling my eyes at Brian.

"You mean he's really here?" said the customer.

"He's as here as you are," said Brian. "What do you want him to do? Move something?"

"Well, why not?" I fretted. "He moves stuff for Erin all the time."

"That's because it gets to her," said Brian. "She loves him."

"Why won't he show himself?" said the customer.

"Hey. Did you leave your underwear in our bathroom?" said Carol.

This prompted a guffaw.

"He says it wouldn't be your *bathroom* he'd leave his underwear in!"

"Oh Lord. I never saw a ghost flirt with a live person," I said.

"He says you never saw a ghost at all!" said Brian.

"Touché," I said. "Brian, does he say what his name actually was?"

"I pick up something with an A. Archie . . . or Archibald is what I keep hearing. He had a really unusual name; it came from his mother's side. And he tells me that when people expect a ghost, that's what they get. That's his job. That's what he was doing at the Crimson Moon. They were expecting a ghost over there, so he gave them one."

"How long has he been doing this?" I said.

"He says it seems like forever."

"Does he want to go on? Leave?"

"He says, '*Hell, no!*' Anyway people wouldn't know

what to do if they didn't have him around. In some ways, it's better than when he was alive," Brian said. "He says he was one of those people that, when people saw him coming, they'd head the other way. Because he loved to talk. Drove people crazy."

"Is he going to let us see him so we can appreciate his looks?" said the customer.

"He says you'll catch him out of the corner of your eye," said Brian. "Spirits aren't for seeing, anyway."

"Well where is he right now?" she said.

Brian walked over and stood in front of her. "He's right here! He's looking at you." Brian paused, then came and stood in front of me. "He says you look tired."

"I'm not tired," I lied. (As usual after a series of readings, I was worn out.) "When did he die, Brian?"

"I believe this man died on December 10, about 1962."

"Is he the one who haunts the second floor of the old Price building?" I asked.

"That's not him," said Brian. "That upstairs draws different people."

"They have a hard time keeping anybody in there," said Carol, referring to the fact that the space was vacant again.

"Well . . . do spirits — does he sleep?" I said, hearing the irony in the question.

"There is no time where he is," said Brian simply.

"So we're talking about a kind of constancy of awareness."

"It's just always now. He's just here." Brian sighed and looked at me. "He's getting tired. Is there anything else?"

"He gets tired?" said the customer.

"Imagine how much energy it's taking to maintain this communication for so long," said Brian. "That's why I can't sit down." It was true that Brian had been moving, just walking around the room, since the session had begun.

"Your energy goes up?" I said.

"And his has to come down, so he and I can meet. Connect."

"Well, let's wrap it up, then. Thanks a lot, Colonel," I said. "We appreciate it."

Brian chuckled. "He says when you get ready to see that saltshaker fly, you call on him!"

It irks me now that I didn't do just that. Why I didn't, I'll never know.

Olde Town Grill, also on the Colonel's beat

a cooler tale

Chase and I met Karen Kunzer when we were having supper at Gabee's downtown and I overheard her telling Charles Mikel ghost stories about her own restaurant, the Olde Town Grill across the street from Jack's Café. The next day I met her at the Grill so she could show me how her ghost had been haunting her kitchen.

When Karen and her sister took over the restaurant last April from the previous owners, they were warned the building was haunted even though it was not even twenty years old. They'd been on the lookout — but they took the rumors all in fun.

Right away I was intrigued to discover that, like so many people who'd had paranormal experiences, Karen was no stranger to ghosts. When she'd lived in a house on the Cape, she'd had a dead sailor for a roommate. "Uncle Ollie" had died in the house an alcoholic, and not, according to the locals, a peaceful soul. Karen knew about him when she moved in, so she wasn't all that surprised when her cabinet doors started banging.

"Probably looking for his liquor," I quipped.

Uncle Ollie also liked to flip the trash can lid up and down. Karen could hear it from the next room.

The roaring fires he sometimes built in the fireplace in the middle of the night were a bit more threatening.

When she and her sister opened the Grill in Dahlonega, it was just little things that happened at first, the kinds of things that made you think your age was catching up with you: a plate where you didn't remember leaving it, a door left open, a pot in the wrong cabinet.

Then the pans started moving around. Nested inside each other, a whole stack of them would suddenly slide off the rack and crash to the floor. Karen would hear the commotion and come running to find only the aftermath: pans everywhere. She wondered whether the changeover of businesses might have created uneasiness; it was something she had felt before. But when activity quieted down for a while, Karen thought her ghost had moved on.

November arrived. Karen was in the restaurant alone, shutting down for the night. She had locked the doors and was getting ready to leave when she heard sounds in her walk-in cooler. She tiptoed into the kitchen and peered around the corner. Slowly, the cooler door opened . . . paused . . . and then, very slowly, closed.

It was a heavy door with a vacuum seal: I saw it myself. There was simply no way it could have opened and closed on its own.

The Psychic Scoop

When I took Brian to the Grill to find out who Karen's kitchen ghost was, it was after closing time, and I expected to have to do our reading from the porch. But as we came through the yard, Karen opened the front door. She had been about to leave, she said, but decided at the last minute to finish one final chore. She was locking the front door when she saw us in the yard.

She invited us into the dining room, and Brian wasted no time telling her that her ghost was none other than that rascal "the Colonel." He liked kitchens, Brian said, but he also liked Karen, and he had given the Grill his seal of approval.

"You can count on business because he's going to help you," said Brian, walking around the room. "He likes your spirit. That's why he moves your stuff around. He says he will bring people down here. You are on his beat."

"Wow. I'm psyched to hear that!" said Karen. "Is there any reason I haven't heard from him in a while?"

"Well, he moved that cooler door," said Brian, "and it spooked a lot of people."

"That's true. I was the only one who wasn't spooked," she said.

"Hey. You didn't tell me that," I said.

"That's why he worked it out so he could talk to you," Brian told Karen. "He doesn't like to scare people. He wants them to feel safe and protected."

I threw out: "Well, he sure scared the life out of Erin Peck."

Brian laughed. "That was different. She didn't mind a good scare!" Then, noticing a picture in an alcove, Brian said to Karen, "You keep that picture there. That's where he stands. He likes it back there."

A few minutes later we were standing in the hall,

surrounded by photographs of Karen's mother and grand-mother and a wall display of her grandmother's hats, when Brian launched into a spontaneous reading for Karen. "This is not for the book," Brian told me quickly, so I can't recount what he said.

What I can say is that in all our time together I'd never seen Brian "read" anyone off the cuff like this, and that what he said to Karen, though it didn't always concern her directly, seemed to carry a kind of urgent significance. And that to my surprise, as Brian was talking to Karen, a chill swept up the back of my neck, and I felt a sudden unaccountable sorrow. I began to cry, and my arms became covered in goose bumps.

This had happened to me once before, when I first began asking around about local ghost stories. When I was shown an authenticated photograph of the apparition of a boy who had died tragically in a train accident a century earlier, I was overcome with tremendous sadness and began to cry. Strangely enough, that story is also one I promised not to pursue, at the request of the woman who owns the old house where the picture was taken. And when I told Brian about it, he believed the owner was (unknowingly) acting as a kind of living representative of the bereaved mother, who even in life was never able to let the dead child go, kept his body with her long past the time when it should have been in the ground, and refused until her dying day to reveal where the boy's grave lay.

Now as Brian and I were leaving Karen's restaurant that evening, I asked him why I'd had such an intense emotional response to both these cases.

He said it was a manifestation of my psychic empathy.

"Those goose bumps are a sign that Spirit is all around you," he said.

"Oh, pooh, Brian. I get goose bumps all the time."

"Well, of course you do," he said kindly, and patted me on the shoulder.

Price building, where a solitary woman waits

the woman who waits
by the window

Built in 1897 by Dahlonega's real colonel, W. P. Price, the Price building has housed Colonel Price's law office, Dr. Head's medical office and drugstore, a grocery store, a theater, and most recently a bakery and café.

I'd heard about a ghost haunting the Price Building's second floor, and Carol Edwards had mentioned that the landlord had a hard time keeping tenants up there. The folks I'd talked to had said it was just that ghostly scallywag "the Colonel" up to his old tricks. Now I wasn't so sure. The Price building wasn't on the Colonel's beat: he'd told us so himself. So who was the presence on the second floor?

The Psychic Scoop

"She was a solitary figure," Brian said, as we stood looking up at the dark windows. "She was manly for her time. Had a Jane Hathaway hairstyle."

"You mean Jane Hathaway from *The Beverly Hillbillies*? Good grief."

"She's that kind of figure . . . but very solitary. She's in that middle window looking down at you — like this." Brian folded his arms and stared down at me from his near seven-foot height.

"Is she mad about something?" I stared hard at the window, trying to see the woman.

"No, she's waiting for someone who's never going to come. It was a strong time in her life, and she just stands there and waits. She doesn't acknowledge anyone; she's not even aware. She's in her own world. That's why the Colonel doesn't go up there." He paused, as though searching for information. Presently he shrugged. "That's all I can pick up. She's just lost and waiting, like an empty room."

"But that's so *sad*," I said. "Can we do anything about it?"

Brian fell quiet a moment. "We can ask for light, but we can't reach her," he said presently. "We just have to move on."

Annabel
comes through the portal

Our friend Cori Lynn was hiking up Black Mountain with Chase and me when she told us about the ghost in the house where she rents rooms a few blocks east of the Square.

Soon after she moved in, her neighbor, who lives on the other side of a hall between the two apartments, told Cori she'd been lying in bed one night when she heard her purse fall off a chair. She got up and put it back. The next night, it happened again. On the third night, she put the purse somewhere else and then her glasses started falling off the dresser. She heard noises in the hallway — not footsteps exactly, but she had a sense that someone was moving around.

Cori had herself heard unexplained noises and felt a breeze when her windows weren't open. She'd felt a presence in her bedroom, but in mid-air, three or four feet off the floor. Lying in bed, she saw a wave of light shoot past.

And sometimes while sitting in the den, she could feel something come up behind her. Her dog Joe would look up and cock his head, but Cori never saw a thing.

Most unnerving, she once heard a loud, clear *"Ahhhhh!"* near her ear — like an exhalation but, as Cori put it, "with a voice behind it."

Cori didn't feel she was in any danger, exactly, but all these sensations were so unsettling that she frequently found herself talking to the presence she sensed so strongly.

"I would ask, you know, 'Can I help you?' or 'Is there something I need to know?' Or when I felt scared, I'd say, 'Please don't do anything bad,' but I never felt threatened. I just didn't feel alone. And that is scary when you can't see anything and you don't know what it is. I mean, for a while I wondered if someone was living in my attic because I heard so much noise."

Over the months that followed, Cori began to feel she understood a little more. She believed the presence was a woman and that her name began with an A. But she couldn't intuit any purpose in the visits. Only once did she have the vague notion that there might have been babies born in the house.

Then one ordinary winter night while Cori was putting laundry away in her bedroom, she saw the ghost standing beside her bed! She was African-American, light-skinned, looked to be in her early twenties, wearing a grayish blue smock-like dress with a light-colored apron.

"She had very pretty features," said Cori, "and her hair was really short and curly, cut close to her head. She didn't seem angry. She was just there." Cori only saw the woman for a fraction of a second, but the image was burned into her memory.

After the ghost's appearance, for no apparent reason activity seemed to subside. By the time I took my recorder to Cori's house to see if the spirit might have anything to say, Cori hadn't felt her presence for some months. The bedroom did take on a kind of foggy quality, similar to what I'd seen in

Rick's attic, and my tape contained a few unusual sounds, but there was too much noise from outside to distinguish the sounds as authentic EVP.

Cori, however, was struck that night with the certainty that the woman's name was Annabel. And after that, activity picked up again.

The Psychic Scoop

Cori couldn't meet with us the next time Brian came to town for readings. Instead, while I was driving him around to Dahlonega's haunted gold mines, I told him about Cori's apparition. Brian said Cori's house was sitting on a kind of psychic open door.

A quartz deposit and trace amounts of gold beneath the house were creating a vortex, he said, and spirits were using the area to pass between the two worlds. The place was a portal!

Cori had been drawn to the house, said Brian, and even to Dahlonega, because she was open to this sort of phenomena, even though it spooked her a little. He was concerned that there might be elementals in the house — either someone she had brought with her from her own family, or a person who had died in the house — drawing Cori's energy and causing health problems.

I mentioned that Cori had felt the house and possibly Annabel herself were somehow associated with babies. But Brian did not believe that Annabel had anything to do with the house at all. "I believe your friend just caught this woman moving between planes," said Brian. "She must have had a great deal of energy. Apparitions are rare."

"Why?"

"Because spirits can't reflect light; their light comes from within. Our eyes are not made to see that. That's when you have to go from eyesight to vision, which is a totally different thing. Perception, imagination, eyesight — vision encompasses all of that. But apparitions take a lot of energy to produce."

"Well, why did things start happening again after our visit?"

"Because everywhere you go, dear, you stir up spirits," he said.

"Oh please, Brian."

"You do stir them up," he insisted, "because you're searching. Your mind is trained on this big question, and that question is vibrating at a frequency that draws its answer to you. So it's drawing these spirits to you — those who want to communicate, and those who want to help you learn and understand."

Now, it scared the fool out of me to think that I might be drawing ghosts wherever Chase and I went . . . especially considering that some of our cemetery visits had been taking place in the dead of night. I told Chase what Brian had said, but I tried not to think about it too much.

Holly Theater, which draws a ghostly audience

a ghostly audience in the Holly Theater

This whole creation is essentially subjective, and the dream is the theater where the dreamer is at once scene, actor, prompter, stage manager, author, audience, and critic.

— Carl Jung
Psychological Reflections

Built in 1948 and restored in the 1990s, the Holly Theater may be a modern building but it shares a reputation for haunts with old theaters all over the world. The Holly has ghosts in the balcony, ghosts in the basement, ghosts on the stage, and ghosts that turn the music on and the lights off and roam among the seats in the auditorium.

"Everyone gets a strange feeling here," the Holly's manager, Colleen Quigley, was telling me as I sat in her basement office drinking coffee one morning.

Maybe everyone but me, I thought. Try as I might, I'd never sensed anything out of the ordinary in the Holly, even when I'd hunted around in the basement one night alone.

Even Colleen, who herself professed not to be "sensitive," had felt a kind of "energy" pushing her out the door when she left the building late. And last summer while rehearsing "Masquerade" from *Phantom of the Opera*, she glimpsed a shadowy figure moving between the seats. The figure was tall, so she thought it was a man.

Not long afterward, Erin Peck was waiting with her husband Jack for a movie to start when the *Phantom* theme song started blaring from the speakers. The sound tech rushed up to the booth, but no one was there. She had just stopped the music when the curtain fell, causing the movie to be postponed for half an hour while the staff hoisted the curtain back up by hand.

Others have had more direct experiences with the Holly's spirited tenants. Gabe Russo, a member of the Holly's community theater cast, was alone in the basement practicing his lines when he glanced toward an interior doorway and saw a tall figure weaving back and forth in a kind of macabre dance. Like Colleen, Gabe thought the figure was a man because of his height, but he couldn't distinguish any features or clothing.

After a moment the figure vanished into the basement, moving through a pile of debris as though it were air.

"I used to be a smart-assed skeptic," said Gabe, "but what I saw down there in the basement changed everything."

Alone in the Holly early one morning, Don McElliott had just swept the steep front stairs from top to bottom and emptied the dustpan. When he started back up to clean the second-floor bathrooms, he almost ran into a chair that had mysteriously appeared in the middle of the staircase.

"But that seems impossible, Don," I said, unable to get the picture in my mind. "You mean the chair was somehow sitting on the steps?"

"Yeah. It was almost like it should have been sliding down."

"But how could it balance?" The idea of a chair in the middle of a flight of steps was so bizarre that I had to have Don, a graphic artist, draw a picture of it for me.

A few weeks later, the water in the unisex bathroom came on and filled up the sink.

The Psychic Scoop

Brian and I sat with our legs dangling off the stage while he introduced me to the standing-room-only crowd of spirits who had gathered at the Holly to "talk" to us. Having heard the buzz on the ghostly grapevine about what we'd been up to around town, these ghosts were eager to find out for themselves what all the fuss was about.

At least that's what Brian said. I found the whole idea absurd, and told him so. He just laughed and for over an hour described some of the people he could "see," while I interposed skeptical commentary, asked questions, or sat quietly amazed at what might, for all I knew, be a real spiritual get-together.

According to Brian, the ghost of Calvin Stone was sitting in seat K-5, near the middle of the room. An older man with a distinguished aspect and a mediator's equanimity, Calvin liked the Holly because it was quiet most of the time and the lights were always buzzing. Calvin was born April 14, 1918, on a farm out toward Cleveland. He went to church, married, had children — but he was best known for his skill as a dowser. He could find water anywhere.

When Calvin died, to his surprise, nothing seemed to change. He didn't feel any different, only time didn't matter any more. He stayed around now to help the others, Brian said, and sometimes acted as a kind of spokesman for the group.

The spirit of a strawberry-blonde woman near the back of the auditorium told Brian that her name was Bessie. She had loved coming to the movies on Saturday afternoons in the Fifties and Sixties, especially to see Susan Hayward. She had lived near where the Wal-Mart is now with her four children, but none of them lived around Dahlonega any more.

A sandy-haired, heavy-set man in a white knit shirt was sitting on the balcony rail, said Brian. Called Ed, or perhaps Jed, he was accustomed to back-door privileges at the Holly from having worked there, owned an interest in the place, or known someone who did. A little over two hundred pounds and not too tall, Ed had liked watching the goings-on downstairs from his perch in the balcony.

"Which one is the Dancing Man Gabe saw in the basement, Brian?" I said.

"That would be this fellow," said Brian, pointing to a seat near the front. "He's standing up. He's tall! He says his name is Allen Hall. He's from downtown Atlanta and he used to come up here camping with his friends on weekends. He died in a car accident on his way home seven or eight years ago. This was the last place he remembered, so he stayed."

"Why was he weaving in the doorway like that?"

"He says he was letting Gabe know there was somebody else down there," said Brian, chuckling. "He couldn't understand why Gabe was making all that noise."

"Well, he was practicing his lines."

"Mr. Hall says, 'Why didn't he have the manners to ask if anybody else was down there?'"

"Well, we don't know any better," I said, looking toward

where Mr. Hall was supposed to be standing. "But we're working on it."

Brian laughed, and so did I (and to my astonishment, when I transcribed the tape later, I clearly heard several other male voices laughing).

Mainly, Brian said, our audience wanted to know what "crossing over " was going to be like. Off the top of my head, I told them I thought it would be a good, light kind of feeling, only multiplied a thousand times. Brian said this was true.

But I was pretty confused about a lot of things. "So when you die," I said to Brian, "you don't see that doorway or portal or whatever it is, with the bright light and the people beckoning you to the Other Side?"

"Not necessarily — unless that's what you're expecting."

"You're saying that if you don't have any ideas about where you're going, or you're too scared to let your mind ask the question, then there's nothing on the Other Side of life except…nothing?"

"Yes…until your consciousness is raised to a level where you begin to ask those questions. Then people come and give you answers."

"But until that time, do you just wander around in the Nothingness? Until you find a place to light?"

"You wander around familiar places. Or you follow vibrations, like the lay lines in the earth. That's magnetic energy."

"So self-development continues even after death," I said. "And your consciousness is not stuck at the point where you die; sooner or later your awareness continues to expand."

"That's right."

"That's very comforting to think about."

"Yes it is. But this is why it's so important for us to talk about death. So we have those images and that connection."

At the moment, a whole host of wandering souls had

"lighted" in the Holly auditorium. There were as many of them as there were seats to sit in, Brian insisted — and then some.

"Then why can't I see them!" I demanded. "If they're really here!"

"Because you're too scared to see them."

"I am not!"

"You are."

He was right, I suppose. I put up a brave front, but it was like Erin Peck had said the night the Colonel froze her in the café. You didn't mind the *idea* of a ghost. You might even get used to spatulas taking flight. But actually *running into* one could scare you out of your wits.

"But what I can't understand is," I pressed, "if these really are just people, what am I so afraid of?"

"All those movies you've seen, with the heads turning around backward and the pig eyes in the windows. Close your eyes, Amy," said Brian. "Move outside your body. Let your imagination show you this theater filled with people — just people. Now take a deep breath, and you'll see some of them turn their heads and look at you. You'll feel a little warmth. It's nothing big or spectacular. It's very subtle."

"I don't feel anything," I complained.

"Well, pretend you do. Just go ahead and ask them if they're ready to leave now."

So I asked them. I asked them if they were ready to have a new adventure. Which was pretty ironic. Considering.

"Oh, they're happy," said Brian. "They trust you."

"But why?"

"Because it's who you are. They love your energy. You bring light to them."

I shook my head. I just didn't know what to make of all this.

"About half of these people are standing up," said Brian,

looking out at the ethereal crowd. "They're getting ready to go. They're excited. It reminds me of an altar call," he said, laughing.

Now Brian and I stood, too, to perform what I had come to think of as a departure ritual. He explained that the process of leaving would seem like going to a train station. The people would start walking into a lighted area, and those who knew them and loved them would be waiting to help them and answer all their questions. They had nothing to fear, and they could change their minds, could even come back if they wanted to; their old seats would still be here.

I told the ones who hadn't stood at Brian's invitation, who wanted to stay behind for a while, that the Holly was surely glad to have them, and if they wanted to show up around the place from time to time, and turn on the water, and weave in the doorways, and move the chairs onto the stairs, I was sure the management would appreciate it.

Brian chuckled. "They said to tell you that if you're watching a show here and you feel something beside you, it will be one of *them*. They do it all the time; people just don't see. *They* didn't see, either. They didn't believe in ghosts themselves...until they became the ghosts!"

the psychic on funeral homes

Where on earth are we?" Brian asked as I drove around looking for a cemetery I'd heard stories about but never been able to find.

"We're back on Highway 60 on the way out of town."

"Are we really? Wow."

"So anyway there's another woman who lives on the other side of the house —"

"Where did you say we were?"

"We're on Highway 60. And anyway this other woman is Spanish, and the Spanish woman — are you listening to me, Brian?"

Brian had rolled down the window and was looking out. "Boy, this is Ghost Central down through here, Amy."

"What?"

"This is Ghost Central!"

"Well, we just went by the funeral home."

"We did? Oh! Now it makes sense."

"What does?"

"Man! People get real interested when their bodies are being made ready for burial. They'll hang around the funeral home sometimes just to watch what's being done to their bodies. And they're very critical sometimes too about how they look or do not look. Wow! That was a trip. Now what were you saying?"

Madeleine Anthony's famous 1953 photo of Mt. Hope cemetery

the ones who watch

In the village cemetery . . . westward from town, there are several rich little veins that show gold freely, and often when digging graves, specimens of quartz sprinkled over with gold are thrown out to view; and the miner has the assurance that when he has laid down his pick and shovel and panned out his last "clean up," his weary bones will be laid to rest within a tomb the walls of which are glittering with the yellow metal for which he toiled all his life away.

— *The Dahlonega Signal*, August 18, 1880

A contingent of Civil War veteran ghosts hangs out on the verandas of the early-1900s-vintage house a few blocks south of the Square, where North Georgia College's Cadet

Recruitment Center keeps its offices. The old men lean against the banisters, sit on the steps, stand in the yard. They like seeing the young recruits coming and going, said Brian. We were walking by the place on the way to the hill in Mt. Hope Cemetery where town librarian and historian Madeleine Anthony had snapped her famous photograph during a Women's Club cemetery clean-up in 1953. Madeleine's camera was aimed at the headstones under a stand of evergreens in one of the oldest parts of the cemetery.

The picture is prized for its apparent depiction of a ghost dressed in period clothing, a great swath of fog on an otherwise clear day, something like part of an early bicycle, and other strange phenomena — but after all the times I've squinted at the picture, I've never been able to conclude that any of this was extraordinary. The ghostly woman looks to me like a fortuitous arrangement of leaves, and the white mist looks like what happens when film is prematurely exposed. I do see a faint image of an early wheeled vehicle, and that's pretty interesting. But I don't see any other ghosts. I was eager to hear Brian's reading at that site.

But to my consternation, once we arrived at the cemetery, I couldn't get Brian to walk up the hill. Instead, he meandered around down below, making idle comments as he read out the names on headstones. "This is where all those old men are buried — the ones on the verandas," he said. It was true that small Confederate flags were waving all over the cemetery beside the graves of soldiers.

He took his time, in no hurry to get where I wanted him to go. "It's up there," I prodded, pointing to the clump of evergreens on the hill.

He glanced at the trees, looked back at me, then wandered to another grave.

"What is it?" I said, frustrated with his slow pace.

"I sense a heaviness up there," he said. "That darkness is

not just under those trees."

That sent a chill up my spine. I hushed.

Brian stopped then and read a name aloud where he stood: "Nicholas Howard, Civil War surgeon," he announced.

The small Confederate flag that should have been beside the grave was lying on its side about ten feet away.

"Wow," said Brian. "This was a hard man to keep down. He threw that flag down so somebody would stop and talk."

"Brian. That could have been the wind, or somebody might have knocked it over or moved it . . ."

"Right," he said, and he looked at me, clearly amused.

I made a huffing sound. "But why would that get anybody's attention?"

"It got ours."

In fact, Nicholas Howard's grave was markedly different from those around it. It was humped up as though it had been dug recently, though the man had died almost a hundred years ago and other graves in the plot had sunk several inches.

"This man's grave is symbolic of his great passion," said Brian. "He was a dedicated healer. I feel that he believes his work is not over, that he still has more to do."

"He was 87. That was pretty old in 1909," I said. (In fact the man must have been well loved, for I found out later that a memorial window in the Methodist Church on Park Street had been dedicated to the memory of *Dr.* Nicholas Fergerson Howard.)

ꝏ

Finally, after more lollygagging around, Brian began to approach the hill where Madeleine's photograph had been taken. He seemed reluctant, and he walked slowly. The shadows under the evergreens were thick even now, in midday. "These people do not want company," he said, shaking his head. "They didn't welcome the camera that day, either."

This early part of the graveyard was dark and fragrant with the scent of rich earth and so old now that some of the headstones were only awkward markers, unreadable and crumbling. The temperature dropped noticeably as we entered the shade. For years, people had been reporting ghosts in this cemetery, and at the moment, I could imagine why.

"This family is territorial about their place in the history of this town," said Brian, walking slowly among the graves. "I feel there was a lot of sadness here. There were way too many premature deaths in this family. Many of these people died young and unfinished."

"Why are they still here?"

"They remain here because they still have a strong sense of ownership, like many of the people in Dahlonega. These were prominent people."

"Castlebury, with B-U-R-Y. It's Castle-B-E-R-R-Y on that road in Auraria," I said.

"I pick up a strong sense of family associated with this name. It's like these people are saying, "We're *here*. We're here to *stay*. And when they let that photograph be taken they were saying: 'We're watching.'"

Cane Creek Baptist Church Cemetery, established 1866

the song of Lizzie Gooch

Our birth is but a sleep and a forgetting:
The Soul that rises with us, our life's Star,
Hath had elsewhere its setting,
And cometh from afar:
Not in entire forgetfulness,
And not in utter nakedness,
But trailing clouds of glory, do we come
From God, who is our home:
Heaven lies about us in our infancy!
— William Wordsworth
"Intimations of Immortality"

Established in 1866, the Cane Creek Baptist Church sits beside its cemetery at the end of a half-mile stretch of isolated road that broaches the southern edge of the Chattahoochee National Forest. I found the place on a whim, when I noticed the sign on the way home one day and decided to have a look at the old church.

The door to the tiny white frame building was unlocked, so I was able to find refuge for a while from a terrifically cold February day. Inside, I sat on old wooden pews and listened to the wind buffet the old building and whistle under the window ledges. I could see the cemetery through the windows.

My first visit to the graveyard was cold and brief. Still, I stayed long enough to become fascinated by three headstones. "Lizzie Gooch" had died in November of 1918 and was buried next to her "infant." As the child also died in 1918, I assumed Lizzie died in childbirth, or perhaps both were victims of the flu epidemic. Lizzie was 26.

On the other side of the baby was the grave of a girl who died in April 1898, two months shy of her 15th birthday. Her name intrigued me: "Tinta Malinda Stargel." Before I left that day, I gathered up a handful of plastic flowers that had blown around the cemetery and placed them on Tinta Malinda's grave.

Although I was fond of cemeteries as a teenager, they have not been a frequent hang-out during my forties. But over the months that followed I found myself drawn back to Cane Creek because I felt a curious attachment to these young people. This sort of thing had never happened to me before. I suppose it was that their stories intrigued me, though I could only guess at how these three had died.

One late-winter day came in cold, but sunny and windless. I took a notebook out to the cemetery, sat down in the grass in front of the three graves, and made some notes. After half an hour, I turned on my recorder and asked some questions, among them: "Lizzie Gooch, I think you died in childbirth. Are you here?" Afterward I repeated the question. "Are you here, Lizzie?"

That night when I played the tape back, for the first ten minutes my questions went unanswered — a familiar response. But then, after my first question to Lizzie Gooch came a moment's silence and then, very faint, but very clear, came the sound of a woman's low singing. The melody had a plaintive quality, and my musician's ear allowed me to make out the six-note phrase well enough to sing it myself.

The next question was answered with more music, introduced by a high, punctuated note that returned to the pitch of the original phrase, but my ears weren't good enough to separate the rest from the white noise generated by the recorder.

I'd read that it wasn't uncommon to hear music or singing on EVP recordings, but I was still struck with wonder. In fact, since the work on this book had begun, despite my skepticism I'd been in a constant state of wonderment. "Freaked out" is how I'd described it to most people. I listened to Lizzie's song over and over again.

Chase and I went back to Cane Creek after midnight on a frigid February night and for half an hour wandered among the headstones recording questions. We stood shivering at Lizzie Gooch's grave, about to leave, when Chase suggested we sing a hymn she might have sung. We sang the chorus from "Shall We Gather at the River," the first verse of "Amazing Grace," and "Wayfaring Stranger," and then we couldn't stand the cold any more and went home.

I played the tape back as soon as we got there, anxious to hear whether Lizzie had spoken this time. To my disappointment, there was no response to any of my questions . . . until we sang "Amazing Grace." I was singing the melody with Chase, but there was a point in the third phrase (*I once was lost, but now am found*) where my voice dropped in pitch. Far off in the background, another voice — a woman's — sang different notes. Someone was singing with us. I was convinced it was Lizzie.

The Psychic Scoop

I could hardly wait to take Brian out to Cane Creek Cemetery, but it was spring before we finally managed to work it into the schedule. Evening was coming in. I took Brian straight to Lizzie Gooch's grave. He nodded. "These are the three that call," he said, indicating Lizzie's, her baby's, and Tinta Malinda's. He looked at me. "You seem to be drawn to the ones with a lot of unfinished business."

"I do?"

"That's why you come here to these. This is an unfinished story." He turned his attention back to Lizzie's headstone. "I don't feel she died *in* childbirth," he said, "but she bled to death soon afterward. That's why she feels so cold sometimes. It was from all the bleeding. And this is a situation where she was warned against the pregnancy. But she wanted this baby."

"What happened to the baby?"

"I feel that it lived a few days. This child outlived its mother. And this energy is one of regret for what it cost these others; that's why it remains here. But this woman is here with this child."

"You mean the *baby* feels regretful? That's hard to swallow, Brian."

"It's almost like this child feels a responsibility — because it wasn't stillborn — that in the little time it was alive it caused all this pain. And this child did not have anybody here on earth because its mother was gone and its father was blaming it for her death, and it was torn, right there in the middle of all that. I think this woman's greatest sadness is how her husband took her death and how he felt toward the baby. It's almost like he wished the baby to die."

"That's awful."

"But he's gone on. He's on the Other Side and where he is now, he understands. I think we need to help her realize that." Brian sighed, and then said, "That's weird, but I'll do it."

"Do what?"

"Well, it's like she understands what I'm saying, but she's been here so long that the earth itself can't let her go."

"You mean the *ground* has got her somehow?"

"The *earth*. These two were commended to the earth, and the earth was charged with the care of these bodies. So I'm going to ask that the vibrations of what is left of these physical bodies be neutralized within the earth and that the earth would forget and settle these vibrations within itself. And I'm going to ask the husband to come and walk this family home. And I'm going to commend these souls to the Creator and Keeper of All Things."

Brian was so serious during all this. I just felt extremely uncomfortable.

"Brian," I said presently, "Why does a spirit stay around its grave as opposed to some other place?"

"Because it's gotten attached to its earthly identity. You don't have that kind of defined identity on the Other Side. That desire for a definite identity gets a lot of people stuck."

"Is Tinta Malinda Stargel here?"

Brian stood a minute, then put his hand to his chest. "She's here. It's getting hard to breathe. There's a pressure in the center of my chest, almost like pleurisy. I think this girl went into a high fever and died and hasn't quite realized what's going on. She's been staying here with these two." He meant Lizzie and the baby. "She says to tell you she loves it when you come out here."

"She does?"

"She doesn't get any visitors," he said. "I believe she was named after an aunt. She wants to know where her mother is buried."

"Tell her I'm sorry. I don't know."

Brian went on to ask that the vibrations of Tinta Malinda's parents and grandparents accompany her to the Other Side. I was quiet, trying to feel reverent and imagine Tinta Malinda reuniting with her mother.

After a few minutes, I wandered off in search of the grave of a preacher I knew was buried out there. "Who else do we need to speak with out here?" I said. I peered at a headstone quickly becoming unreadable in the fading light. A pair of whippoorwills had set up a racket in the woods.

"There's a lot of energy around that Ridley plot," said Brian.

"There's a preacher out here somewhere. Lots of soldiers. I'm always interested in military men."

"That's because you've been so many yourself. That's why you give orders. You have a big Civil War past life."

I ignored this. Not that I didn't believe reincarnation happened; it seemed perfectly reasonable to me. But anybody could make up a fictitious life.

"I've lost track of that preacher — wait," I said. "Here he is. Reverend John J. Stargel." His grave was not far from Tinta Malinda's.

Brian came over and put his hand on the headstone. "Do you know why this grave draws you?" he said after a minute. "You knew this man. In the Indian Wars."

"I did?"

"You were on earth as a man then, and you either commanded him or served with him. You knew him well. He was a friend."

"Imagine finding his grave."

"It was a blessing," said Brian.

Suddenly a whippoorwill sailed out over the graves, then disappeared into the trees and set up a curious chirping sound. A second whippoorwill followed, lighted on a head-stone, then flew back into the woods.

"Did you see that?" I said, stunned. The whole thing had been like a performance.

"You just don't see those birds," said Brian, shaking his head. "Whippoorwills are extremely aloof."

"*Two* whippoorwills. I've heard them all my life. Never seen one."

"Neither have I."

Darkness was settling in. Brian seemed anxious to leave.

"Are you worried about something?" I said.

"Not really worried . . . but we should go."

"Don't tell me *you're* scared of graveyards at night!"

Brian laughed. "It's not that. But we've been up on a high vibration, doing all these readings, and when it begins to grow late, the energies here grow, too. It's easy to lose touch with your grounding in the earth plane, and you're much more susceptible to float out there, get lost between the two worlds."

"Well, Chase and I have been in cemeteries lots of nights when it was really late. Nothing has ever happened to us."

"Take my word for it. That's the time when mortals should *not* be walking around in cemeteries. Twilight, sundown, that's okay. After that, you want to keep your distance."

∾

Several months later I discovered that the Reverend John Jones Stargel had been born in North Carolina in 1813. Orphaned at age 3, he came to Georgia as a young man, married, and had thirteen children. During his twenties he served as a First Lieutenant in the Georgia Militia and fought in the Indian Wars, then became a farmer and the minister of Cane Creek Baptist Church. He died in 1874 at the age of 61. He was Tinta Malinda Stargel's paternal grandfather.

Tinta Malinda succumbed to an unspecified illness that lasted only a few days. According to the obituary printed in the *Dahlonega Nugget*, she was arranging a cup of flowers when she said to one of her four sisters: "I want you to sit this at my grave when I die."

Lizzie Gooch, born Sarah Elizabeth Stargel, was one of those sisters. She was not quite 9 years old when Tinta Malinda died. She and her husband, Garland Andrew Gooch, had just celebrated their first anniversary in September 1918. Six weeks later, she died — and then, according to Brian, the baby. The father was left on his own. If the family tree I found on the web is correct, he was 7 years younger than Lizzie and would have been only 19 when she and the baby died.

Tinta Malinda's mother, also named Sarah, is buried in town at Mt. Hope Cemetery.

my dog Floyd talks to the psychic

My dog Floyd took up with me seven winters ago when I was living in rural Kansas. He was at least two years old and a starved wraith of a dog then, with a scraggly coat and a cowering manner. Months went by before he'd let me get close enough to touch him.

Now he's a beauty, with the golden fur of a Sheltie and the blazed face of a Malamute. He's terrified of brooms, fly swatters, and men, especially if they are loud or sudden. He positively despises cigarette smoke and goes in another room if anyone lights a match. He loves potato chips and vanilla wafers.

Now, Brian didn't know much about Floyd except that I'd taken him in as a stray. But Brian liked Floyd immensely. When Floyd rode around with us in the car, Brian was always talking to him, complimenting him and patting him on the head. "You're so *polite*, Floyd," he'd say dramatically. "You have a *beautiful* coat."

One day while the three of us were riding around deciding where to do our next reading, Brian piped up,

"Your dog wants to know if there's anything you'd like to ask him."

"Oh please, Brian."

"Your hair matches his, he thinks. He loves that about you."

I snorted and rolled my eyes. "I'd better not stop using the highlighter, then." I thought a minute. "Hey, ask him what his life was like before he showed up at my door."

"He was dropped off," said Brian. "He was given to a woman as a gift, but whoever the man was with her didn't relish her giving the dog more attention than he got."

"Well, it's true that he doesn't do well with men."

"That's because that man stuck him in a car and drove off with him. And that man smoked. He smoked a lot."

"Floyd hates cigarette smoke."

"And that's what he remembers, how the cigarette smoke was filling up the car. And the man just opened the door and threw the dog out and off he drove. Floyd says he lived on his own a long time. He was a good hunter."

"For such a good hunter, he sure didn't eat much," I said. Floyd was half his current weight when he showed up at my house.

"He says he survived. He loved being on his own. He's only polite on the leash because it makes you happy. He knows how important it is that he be polite and well-mannered, because you've told him."

"Oh, brother. Brian, don't tell me dogs can *talk*."

Brian looked at me. "Your dog does."

"That's crazy."

"It's not *language*; it's thought forms, feelings, pictures — everything put together at once. I can tell that you talk to Floyd a lot, because he communicates in complete ideas. Now, a wild animal that doesn't have much human contact will be aware of me there, but it doesn't have a set of symbols or images that it shares with me. So I can only pick up that animal's awareness. We teach our animals language just like we teach our children to talk."

"Can animal spirits become ghosts?"

"Only if their owners won't let them go."

"Do they reincarnate?"

"Yes, but they only change animal form: a dog can come in as a cat or a monkey or a moose. They don't come back as people. And people don't return as animals."

"Do animals have conscious awareness?"

"Yes. And telepathic awareness. That's how they know what you're going to do before you know it."

"Hey. I have a friend who rescues animals and she has twenty-six cats and dogs right now. Maybe we should go out to her house and see what happens."

"Ha," said Brian. "They'd all come up and talk at once."

I corrected him. "It's not really *talking*, though."

He threw me an amused look. "Right."

scary ghosts, evil, & possession

"Brian, why do apparitions or paranormal events sometimes appear so horrific, like blood running down walls or dead flesh hanging everywhere? Why do ghosts try to scare you?"

"That's Hollywood. That's not real."

"So when *you* see an entity —"

"When I see an entity, even if it's somebody who has been mangled —"

"Like the motorcycle guy at Rick's."

"I'm sure his physical form was pretty roughed up. But the etheric body does not hold those wounds. That's material. When you see blood running down walls and zombies and vomit, that's Hollywood."

"But what about all the people who've reported seeing those things?"

"They've seen hallucinations. They're already scared, and their minds are pulling up scenes from every horror movie they've ever watched. But that is not real."

"Is there such a thing as evil?"

"Evil as an incarnate being, no. Evil as ego and pride, yes. Evil is a force created by someone living. It does not exist on its own. It is not a free-floating thing that floats in and willy-nilly grabs you."

"I got a letter from a woman who was worried that bad things were going to happen to me because of my work on this book. What does that fear stem from?"

"From a religious ignorance that keeps people from stepping into areas religion doesn't have answers for. So the paranormal has been made taboo, something to fear. We make taboos out of all kinds of things we don't understand or aren't at peace with, rather than deal with our own discomfort. The woman who wrote to you has these gifts and she's terrified of them. If you use *your* gifts and nothing bad happens to you, she's going to have to revamp her entire belief system. So she needed to stop you so she wouldn't have to change what she believed."

"She was afraid I might become possessed."

"People are always afraid they're going to run into something like the Amityville Horror and need an exorcist. But they need to realize that before one of those manifestations occurs, someone has spent an awful lot of time drawing that energy to them. It isn't something that can just come upon them; it has to be focused, directed, and invoked. There are no evil demons that twist their heads around and spit at you and possess people. That's Hollywood."

Park Street home of "Walter" and his cat

I see a ghost on Park Street

Only with the sense that the world is not solid is it possible to move.

—Bob Perelman
a.k.a.

I was escorting Brian down Park Street because I wanted to show him an old white two-story house that gave me the creeps. I never saw a light on so I thought it was deserted, and I was standing in the front yard one night, trying to record EVP, when I was sure I heard someone walking toward me through the grass, though I never saw a soul. It scared me so badly I ran all the way to my car.

On the way to the white house, Brian and I stopped at Colonel Price's house for a reading. Brian assured me that the colonel himself — Colonel *Price* — was watching us from the porch. "Dahlonega is full of old men who won't give up," Brian said. "The judge still rules his courthouse. Mr. Strickland looks after his house. Colonel Price is here, too, proud of the contribution he made. But he's not stuck here, and he wants everybody to know that. He's just here. He says to please tell the owner thanks for taking care of *his* house. There's nothing to do here."

"Brian, how do I know whether to believe what you're saying to me?" I said, grappling as usual with the questions I never could resolve. "How does anybody know whether to believe any of this?"

"Because the truth resonates," he said. "You know when somebody's bullshitting you and when they're telling you the truth. Don't you?"

I thought about this. "Usually," I said. But not always, I added silently.

We walked on until I stopped at a white house on the corner. "It's the upstairs and the front yard," I said, indicating the small balcony. "I feel a heaviness there. A sadness. It just disturbs me to look at it. And one night I was trying to record EVP in the front yard and I could have sworn somebody walked right up to me."

"Close your eyes and tell me. Is it a man or a woman?"

I rolled my eyes. "Oh, Brian, you know I don't do this stuff."

"But you *can* do it. What's going through your mind?"

I closed my eyes and tried to let down my many defenses, but saw nothing and felt nothing unusual. "I think I do better when I'm talking," I said.

"Keep talking, then. 'I feel that this is a . . .'"

I huffed. "I don't know."

"No, you don't know. Relax. You feel there's a heaviness."

"Right. On the second floor. It seems like a man."

"That's right."

"It is?" Well, it was fifty-fifty odds.

"Is he a big man?" said Brian.

I closed my eyes again and sought an image. Instantly, a picture formed in my mind, so I described it. "He's middle-aged. Fortyish, sort of tall. Has a paunchy middle. He's not very healthy. He's bent over, shaped sort of like an S. Got thinning hair, graying, and he's wearing a white shirt and dark gray pants. He's terribly unhappy. I mean, the sense I have of him is just very negative."

"What is he doing?"

"Nothing. He's just standing here in front of me with his head down."

"Now, reach into your mind and ask him to tell you why he's sad. Imagine the words leaving your mind and going to him. And then listen inside yourself. See if any images come from your own life of the times you were sad, or if a scene comes up inside you. Because whatever scene or idea that comes to you next, no matter what you think of it, will be that man telling you why he's sad. This is how he relates to you: through your own experiences."

I kept my eyes closed to help filter out distractions and waited a long time, trying to empty my mind of anything that might be me trying to think something up that might sound good. After a few minutes, the word *cat* kept repeating itself in my mind, but it wasn't attached to any image of *cat*. I told this to Brian. "What does that mean?" I said.

Brian shrugged. "Ask him."

I thought: "What about your cat?" to the man, and again, I waited. For a long time, nothing came. I opened my eyes and walked a few paces forward into the yard, and then I looked toward the azaleas at the corner of the house and saw a large gray tabby cat sitting very still. "That's too strange for words," I said to Brian. I had not noticed the cat before.

Brian nodded. "But what about *his* cat? Why is he so disturbed?"

Again I waited, and soon I felt a wave of sadness associated with the idea of *cat*. "There's just a tremendous sadness. I don't know why."

"Ask him if he'll tell you why."

I waited. "His cat was run over," I said presently, trying to ignore how unimaginative it sounded. "He found it after it was already dead. He was very upset." The images were coming faster now. "The cat was very important to him. He lived alone."

"Will he let us help him go to where his cat is?"

I thought the words to the man. "He looked up!" I said, startled.

"That's a yes," said Brian.

"He looked up at me. He's got this hopeful look." My arms were suddenly covered in goose bumps.

"Good. You're in channel. Stay with yourself. Ask him to repeat after you so you can help him leave."

Oh, but I was into it now. I asked the man to tell me his name, and I could see his mouth move in reply, but I couldn't hear what he was saying. "He's trying to communicate something to me, Brian, but it's like he can't say the word out loud. The word is inside him, in his mouth, but it doesn't come out, and his mouth moves but it's like there's no breath. Or no vocabulary."

"What do you feel on the inside?"

"I'm not certain enough to say."

"Then pretend you're certain. Just say the sound that comes into your mind."

"It's a *waah* sound, like maybe Walter."

"Okay. I was picking up Arthur, or Roger. You're saying Walter. It's an inexact science. Let's go with Walter. Now ask him to repeat after you."

In my mind, I told Walter that if he wanted to join his cat, he could say the words I said to him and go to a place where he wouldn't be alone any more. Then I repeated what Brian told me to say. "'I'm ready to go now,'" I prompted Walter. "'I want to go where the light is bright . . . I want to go where my cat is . . . I want to go *now*.'"

During this departure ritual, I saw Walter turn around. There was a light in the distance behind him, and a cat silhouetted in that light. "He sees his cat!" I said.

"Send him on with a blessing of peace, then," said Brian.

I did, and Walter walked into the light with his cat beside him, just like in the movies.

"He's happy now," said Brian. "He's not alone any more."

I frowned. "I don't know. I have a healthy imagination."

"That's good. That's the reason you can be used in this way. They don't call in people with no imagination to do soul retrieval work."

I didn't ask who "they" was. I just assumed he meant some spiritual committee over there on the Other Side. "But Brian," I said, "how do I know I didn't just make Walter up? I'm a storyteller. It's what I *do*."

"Amy, would you please just stand out in the yard and *receive*? You have to learn to trust yourself. You are not your parent. You're not trying to contrive an image and then hide something behind it. You just helped somebody go where he needed to go. It was real. It was true. *It was all over you.*

"Listen," he went on. "The imagination has been so misunderstood. We say, 'Oh, I made all that up so it isn't real.' But the imagination is about *images*. When the spirits talk with me, I might have the sense of a woman. In my mind, I'll imagine a generic female figure. But then that generic picture will begin to take on individual aspects. Still,

I give the image a form with my mind. Your imagination is your connection with the spirit realm. And that connection is real."

"But Brian. Where's the discernment? What if I told you that there was a little girl in the house down the street who had died from neglect and now she's hanging out down there waiting for her mother to come tell her she loves her. But I made that up. It's not true."

"Well, you know you made that up, don't you?"

"Of course."

"So you don't question it, do you."

"No. But —"

"This is the rule. If you catch yourself questioning something — like Walter, for instance — then trust it. It's authentic. If you'd made it up, you'd know it."

"But are you saying, then, that my imagination can't do something on its own? That there has to be some will involved?"

"Exactly."

"Well what about dreams?"

Brian shook his head. "That's a whole different level of consciousness. Not the same thing at all."

We left the conversation there and walked on down toward the end of the street. I pointed to another vacant house where I'd heard a loud cracking sound from the porch in response to a question I'd asked during another of my attempts to record EVP. Floyd had been with me, whining incessantly. I asked Brian about it.

"Whoever built that house is still in there," he said. "Again, it's that possessiveness in Dahlonega. This person knew you were out here searching, but he wanted you to keep moving. When the dog whines, Amy, walk on."

We stopped at a last house, a small one near the bottom of the hill.

"This house seems dark," I said. I was talking about the energy, not the color.

Brian took one look at the place and took off walking, which when you're six-foot-eight is a pretty fast pace. "That house holds secrets it doesn't want anybody to know," he said. I was moving fast, trying to catch up with him.

"So we don't read that one?"

"We do not psychically connect."

"Why not?"

"When I'm told it's none of my business," he said, "I move my being on down the way."

"But you said ghosts can't hurt us," I said, practically running to keep up, he was walking so fast.

"No, they cannot physically hurt you."

"Can they hurt us emotionally?"

He stopped and looked at me. "They can trip us into our own hysteria, our own fear. The only place a ghost has any power is in the mind. That's why you must be very confident and know what you're doing when you step into this work, because otherwise it can turn around on you. You have to stay clear inside yourself."

"So if you feel you can't handle it —"

"You leave!"

Historic marker at Auraria

cleansing the fort at Auraria

During the last few months Brian was working with me I asked him if he would mind going out to the site of the old fort at Auraria, where the Cherokees were confined until they embarked with U.S. military escorts to Oklahoma on what became known as the Trail of Tears. I wondered what kind of psychic signals he would pick up in those woods.

Now covered by forest, the site was heavily mined after the Indians left, and the land is gouged with deep holes and the raised tracks of old road beds.

Brian was quiet as he approached the place. I hung back, not knowing what to expect, and not wanting to disturb him. It was afternoon and chilly, and the place was eerily hushed.

"First thing I'm picking up is stoic resignation," he said. "The pride of the Cherokee people. And the numbness of their spirits — that this was happening to *them*. You can feel their presence — the oppressive energy right on top of this hill. It just holds you down." He looked at me. "This is a place where crying would not help," he said. "And they didn't cry. The Trail of Tears — they were not their tears, but the tears of those watching them pass by. And while the people are not here now, their presence is recorded in the earth and the stones and trees. That's why the animals are silent. They're all off in the distance."

I said nothing, pondering the words.

"I feel the broken will," he went on. "The lost hope. Almost a helplessness: 'What can you do?'" He sighed. "Wise people. Brilliant people, knowing exactly what was going on, the way they stood and waited and watched, doing the best they could to get the children and the women into the middle."

After a moment, he raised a hand toward the sky, offering tobacco. "Spirit of these woods," he said, "we offer this tobacco for that which was done here. We have come to cleanse this land so you can breathe again. We have come to free you from all that has held you. In the prayer language of the Siksika…[here he spoke a long string of Blackfoot words, a language of sibilants, hard *k* sounds, and short vowel sounds]. On behalf of the whites who did this to you," he was saying, "I offer this tobacco to you. For the years you have spent in agony, I offer this tobacco to you. For your healing, Mother Earth, rise, and let this pain and this atrocity be forever swallowed and gone, and let this earth again know life and light."

Finally he fell quiet. After a few minutes we turned to leave, and in that moment a red-tailed hawk flew over, calling, and the sound echoed through the woods behind us as we walked away.

Window in the old city jail under the Corkscrew Café

When you understand that this present life is only one day in your long life, and that at the change called death you simply disappear into the next plane, to come back again later — or perhaps several hundred years later — then the events of this particular life appear in their true proportion, and then you begin to have dominion. The events of this life will not appear less important because of your new knowledge, but they will no longer intimidate you, because you will know that you can control them. No seeming misfortune will any longer have power to break your heart or weaken your courage. You will understand life as the wondrous opportunity and the glorious gift that it is.

— Emmet Fox
Around the Year with Emmet Fox